Fifty Ways
to
Resist the Devil

Strategies for
Dealing with Satanic Attacks
in Key Areas of Life

Dr. William R. Glaze

Qoheleth Publishing

Fifty Ways to Resist the Devil: Strategies for Dealing with Satanic Attacks in Key Areas of Life
by Dr. William R. Glaze
Copyright © 2016 Dr. William R. Glaze

ISBN 978-1-63360-029-4
For Worldwide Distribution
Printed in the U.S.A.

ACKNOWLEDGMENTS

I would like to give glory to God for allowing me to write this book. I would also like to thank my wife Angie, who got me started on the path to writing it. Finally, I would also like to thank Marie Franklin, Linda Savido, Sharon Strong, Toya West, Sheila Adams and Lorraine Perry for proofreading and checking out the scriptural references.

TABLE OF CONTENTS

HOW TO USE THIS BOOK

This book is written in short vignettes with the biblical reference, a brief exegesis of the passage, a succinct lesson on how to deal with the devil, a thoughtful conclusion and a prayer. It can be used in several ways. First, it is recommended that one peruse it and become familiar with the content. Second, there is a subject index in the back of the book. The reader can go to a specific topic and read what it has to say about dealing with Satan in that area. Third, it can be used in a Bible-study setting to address the issue of spiritual warfare with the devil. Fourth, a children's teacher can work with the material and creatively design age-appropriate lessons for youth. However, it should be kept in mind that all subjects may not be suitable for children.

INTRODUCTION

A humorous story is told about a man who was "trick or treating" one Halloween night dressed as the devil when all of a sudden he got caught in a bad thunderstorm. On the same night in that town a church was having a revival. To get out of the rain, the man in the devil's costume darted into the church. As the pastor was preaching, he froze in the middle of his sermon when he saw the man dressed as the devil enter the rear of the sanctuary. The look on the pastor's face caused the people sitting in the pews to direct their attention to the back of the church. As the man in the costume made his way down the aisle, everyone in attendance began to run out of the building. One lady attempting to flee got her dress caught on the end of the pew. As he walked toward her she stuttered as she exclaimed, "I- I-I, been in the church for over thirty years, bah-bah-bah, but I've been serving you the whole time." This amusing story serves as a good reminder that the devil is alive and well; and not only that, he is also busy in the church among God's people.

The devil is frequently depicted as wearing a red skin-tight suit, with pointed ears, a tail and carrying a pitchfork. This caricature has caused many to not take him seriously and some

Christians do not believe he really exists. To the contrary, the Bible clearly proves Satan is real and one of his objectives is to take down and destroy God's children. With that thought in mind, this book has been written to help believers identify the work of the devil in their lives and how to effectively deal with him.

It is not the objective of this book to blame everything on Satan or to say, in the words of Flip Wilson, a comedian of past times, "The devil made me do it." Sometimes we are victims of our own sinful devices or we reap the fruits of a fallen human nature. However, throughout the Bible we see the devil at work in devious ways. Therefore, the objective of this book is to look at those occasions in which he is manifested and see what believers can learn from those biblical records in the fight against this ancient foe.

Back in the 1970s Paul Simon sang a song titled: *Fifty Ways to Leave Your Lover.* The chorus of the song went something like this, "Slip out the back Jack. Make a new plan Stan." I've always wondered why he only gave six ways to leave your lover when he said there were fifty ways. Whatever the case, in this book, I have listed more than fifty ways to resist the devil. As you read these different ways may the Lord give you the strength and wisdom to "stand against the wiles of the devil."

PROTECT YOUR HOME, JEROME

*"Now the serpent was more subtle than
any beast of the field which the LORD
God had made. And he said unto the
woman, Yea, hath God said, Ye shall not
eat of every tree of the garden?"*
Genesis 3:1

We have a record in the Bible of how God used Adam and Eve to establish the first home. After they were created, God placed them in a perfect environment called the Garden of Eden. The word "Eden" (Hebrew *ay-den*) means delight; the Garden of Eden was a place of happiness, pleasure and enjoyment. Unfortunately, the devil, in the form of a serpent, entered this utopia and introduced sin into the world by getting the first couple to doubt the Word of God and eat the forbidden fruit. From that point until the present time he has been at the root of the majority of disturbances in the home.

The range of problems created by Satan in the home have been enumerable—lack of communication, disrespect, unresolved issues, outbursts of anger, infidelity, all types of abuse, addictions, financial problems, rebellion, and

1

the list goes on. One way to guard your home—Jerome, is to put the Lord at the center of it. The Bible says in Psalm 127:1, *"Except the LORD build the house, they labour in vain that build it."* A house built upon the Lord is one where the Word of God is at the center of it and the family worships together both privately and publicly. Failure to do this leaves a crack for the serpent to slither through and wreak havoc in the home.

Be aware, the snake got into the first home and he has been trying to get into homes ever since then.

Prayer

Dear Heavenly Father, please put a hedge of protection around my home and keep it safe from the attacks of the enemy. Help me to know and to do the things which help to build a godly home.

DON'T GET A BIG HEAD, FRED

*"And Satan stood up against Israel, and
provoked David to number Israel."*
1 Chronicles 21:1

David was king over Israel and God used him in mighty ways to subdue their enemies. On one occasion, Satan put a thought into David's head to count all of the fighting soldiers. This was not the will of God because it would cause David to turn from trusting God to trust in his military power. The psalmist said, *"It is better to trust in the Lord than to put confidence in man"* (Ps. 118:8). The devil fed into David's ego and enticed him to number the army. As a result of his self-centeredness, God sent a judgment that took the lives of 70,000 people (1 Chron. 21:14).

The people of God have to be careful that they are not putting their confidence in the wrong objects. We can be like David and let Satan draw us into something that takes us away from trusting God. It can be in our ability to memorize Bible verses, the eloquence of our prayers, the ability to manage money or the gift to lead praise and worship. Whatever we do, we must be humbly dependent upon the Lord.

Placing trust in our gifts and talents can cause us to get a big head, Fred.

A humble heart keeps us from getting a big head.

Prayer

Lord, help me to trust You in all my ways and not give a place for the devil to work in my life by leaning to my own understanding.

SEEK GOD EARLY, PEARLY

"And the Lord said unto Satan, Hast thou considered my servant Job, that there is none like him in the earth, a perfect and an upright man, one that feareth God, and escheweth evil?" Job 1:8

In the passage recorded above God is bragging about Job to Satan. In this one verse he says four things about Job's spiritual life: (1) He is perfect (Hebrew word *tawm* meaning blameless); (2) He is upright, one who walks in righteousness; (3) He feared God or had a reverential respect for the Lord; and (4) He eschewed evil or turned away from wickedness.

Upon hearing this, Satan said the reason for Job's holy life was because God put a hedge around him (Job 1:10). He further went on to say that if God removed the hedge, Job would curse God to his face (Job 1:11). After this we read that Satan viciously attacked Job. But he was able to withstand the Satanic assaults because he was rooted and grounded in a relationship with the Lord. In verse 5 we read that Job had a continual practice of worshipping God. Each morning he would rise up early and offer sacrifices. Job realized the importance of meeting with God so he rose up early to have a quiet time. This is an encounter with God where time is spent in Bible reading and prayer. You can do this at any time during the day, but, it is probably best to do it early, Pearly.

Our day will be brighter and our load will be lighter when we seek God early.

Prayer

Father, help me to rise early each morning and pause before entering the day, to take time to read my Bible, study it and pray.

HOLD ON TO YOUR PRAISE, BLAISE

"The workmanship of thy tabrets and of thy pipes was prepared in thee in the day that thou wast created." Ezekiel 28:13

In this verse we read about Lucifer, the devil's name before he fell from Heaven. He had an awesome ability to praise God with tambourines (*tabrets*) and flutes (*pipes*). One day sin was found in him and he was not only cast out of the garden of God, he lost his job of praising the Lord. I heard one preacher say, "God created the devil to praise Him and he lost his job! Now he is mad because we have his job. The devil does not want your house, your car or your clothes; he wants your praise."

God wants man to praise Him. In Psalm 107 it says four times, "Oh that men would praise the Lord" (8, 15, 21, 31). Whenever God says something one time it is important but if He says it more than once we should take extra special note of it. It is not hard to praise the Lord because there are so many things we can praise Him for—who He is, what He does, and all He has done for us personally. Just like Satan lost his job of praising God, we can lose ours if we fail to praise Him. Jesus said if people hold their praise that "*the stones would immediately cry out*" (Lk. 19:40). One song writer wrote, "Ain't no rocks gonna cry in my place, as long as I am alive to glorify his holy name." The psalmist said, "*The dead praise not the Lord, neither any that go down in silence. But we will bless the Lord from this time forth and for evermore. Praise the Lord*" (Ps. 115:17-18). Hold on to your praise, Blaise, and don't let the devil steal it.

Bless the Lord at all times and let His praise continually be in your mouth.

Prayer

Dear God, please keep me mindful of the fact that whatever I go through, I can find a reason to praise You!

PUT ASIDE PRIDE, CLYDE

"Thine heart was lifted up because of thy beauty, thou hast corrupted thy wisdom by reason of thy brightness: I will cast thee to the ground, I will lay thee before kings, that they may behold thee."
Ezekiel 28:17

In Ezekiel 28 we read about a character identified as "the king of Tyrus" (12). Many believe this is a veiled reference to Satan before he fell from Heaven. There are several characteristics recorded about this individual. He was perfect in wisdom (12), beauty (12-13a), music (13b) and in every way (15). He had access into the presence of God; he was in the garden of God (13), the holy mountain of God (14) and the sanctuaries of God (18). He was the anointed cherub, a designation for a powerful angel (14). What a magnificent creature!

However, a serious flaw arose in his character and that was pride. In verse 17 we see his heart was lifted up with pride because of his beauty and his wisdom. For this reason he was cast out of the mountain of God to the ground, brought to ashes and laid before kings (16-18). Jesus was an eyewitness to the fall of Satan from

9

heaven. In Luke 10:18 He said, "*I beheld Satan as lightning fall from heaven.*"

The devil is the author of pride and when it is found in us we open a door for him to come and work in our lives. We can be victimized by several types of pride and they are epitomized in the following statements. "Everybody look at me." "Protect my ego at all costs." "I am the greatest." "I will not be the first to give in." "I did not get the recognition I deserved." "Nobody can tell me what to do."

We must remember, Satan can take our prideful attitudes and bring about destructive results. The Bible says pride goes before the fall (Prov. 16:18) and it brings shame (Prov. 11:2). One of the fifty ways to resist the devil is to put aside pride, Clyde.

The antidote for pride is to be HUMBLE: Helpful, Understanding, Meek, Broken, Loving, Empathetic.

Prayer

Most gracious Lord, please make me aware of pride when it creeps into my life. Give me the wisdom to fight pride with humility.

LOOK OUT FOR THE DEVIL'S EYE, TYE

"Thou hast defiled thy sanctuaries by the multitude of thine iniquities, by the iniquity of thy traffick." Ezekiel 28:18

In Ezekiel 28:11-19 we read about a prophecy concerning the king of Tyre, but the reference goes far beyond this historical point in time. It takes us all the way back to a time when Satan, who was created a perfect being named Lucifer, lived in Heaven. He became corrupted and was expelled from the garden of God. Ezekiel gives us one of the reasons for his fall when he records the following phrase "by the iniquity of thy traffick." The word "traffick" referred to someone who peddles or tries to sell goods to others. When he was in Heaven, Satan tried to sell his program of rebellion against God to other angels.

Television programs can be a wonderful tool. There are many educational programs that increase our learning, spiritual programs that minister to our spirits and news programs that keep us informed about the things going on in the world. But the television can also be a place

11

where the devil peddles his goods of ungodly programing, seductive commercials and immoral relationships. Years ago I heard someone refer to the television as the "devil's eye." Today the devil's eye can extend far beyond the television. It can refer to anything that has a screen— smart phones, tablets, laptop computers, desktop computers, and the multitudes of gaming devices. These things can be used for good or for evil, and that is why it is important to be aware of the devil's eye, Tye.

A television can become a great resource for relaxation and information, but don't allow it to become the devil's eye.

Prayer

Heavenly Father, please allow the Holy Spirit to convict my heart when I am viewing things that are not pleasing to You or when I am spending too much time in front of a screen.

DISCARD THE HOROSCOPE, HOPE

"Then the king commanded to call the magicians, and the astrologers, and the sorcerers, and the Chaldeans, for to shew the king his dreams. So they came and stood before the king." Daniel 2:2

Nebuchadnezzar was the king of Babylon who destroyed the southern nation of Judah in 586 BC. As a result, he took some of the best and brightest Hebrew young men into captivity. One night he had a dream that troubled him. The next day he summoned the magicians, astrologers and the sorcerers to see if they could not only interpret his dream but also tell him the dream itself. To make a long story short, none of them were able to do what he asked except a young Hebrew named Daniel. After seeking God, he was not only able to tell the king what he dreamed, but also its interpretation. His powers and abilities came from God but the Babylonian magicians, astrologers and sorcerers received their power and abilities from one of two places—self or Satan.

In light of God's condemnation of similar professions in Deuteronomy 18:10-12, it can be safely concluded that they were energized by Satan. To further confirm this truth, the Apostle

13

Paul said to a sorcerer in the New Testament, "*O full of all subtilty and all mischief, thou child of the devil, thou enemy of all righteousness, wilt thou not cease to pervert the right ways of the Lord?*" (Acts 13:10). Paul called this sorcerer a child of the devil who sought to corrupt the righteousness of God.

Astrology is trusting the arrangement of the stars in the heavens to ascertain one's destiny and how he should view the events of each day. In a sense this is worshipping the stars, a practice expressly forbidden by the Lord (Deut. 4:19). The horoscope is based on astrology and no child of God should in any way dabble in this practice. Given the fact that this is energized by Satan, it attempts to transfer the believer's trust in God to the alignment of the stars. This is good reason for you to discard the horoscope, Hope.

Rather than looking to the stars to find your future, why not look to God, the star's creator?

Prayer

Father, give me discernment and let me not fall prey to the unsuspecting allurement of worshipping the creation instead of the Creator.

DO NOT PRESUME, BOOM

"Then the devil taketh him up into the holy city, and setteth him on a pinnacle of the temple, and saith unto him, If thou be the Son of God, cast thyself down: for it is written, He shall give his angels charge concerning thee: and in their hands they shall bear thee up, lest at any time thou dash thy foot against a stone."
Matthew 4:5-6

When the devil tempted Jesus in the wilderness, he took Him to a high point on top of the temple and told him to jump off. Then the devil went on to make an assumption that God would send angels to catch Him before He crashed upon the rocks below. The devil was presumptuously quoting Psalm 91:11-12. Jesus responded to the devil's challenge by saying that no one should tempt God, which is a quote from Deuteronomy 6:16. To tempt God is to challenge Him to do some supernatural feat to prove who He is. There are times that God tells us to do something to test Him (Mal. 3:10), but when we presumptuously dare God to do something, that is tempting Him.

One of the meanings of presume in Webster's dictionary is to dare. When we dare someone, we are challenging them to do something to prove they can do it. Sad to say, there are some believers who have taken the devil's offer to presume upon God. They falsely believe they are trusting God by faith to work in a particular situation, when they are in essence exercising presumption. I have heard many of the saints say they are trusting God to help them win the lottery. The Bible is very clear that it is not God's Will for His people to gamble. Therefore, for a person to say they are trusting God to win the lottery is not faith but presumption. The next time you say you are trusting God for a blessing, make sure you do not presume, Boom.

Instead of putting faith in God, presumption means that we want God to put faith in us.

Prayer

Father, grant me the wisdom to know the difference between faith and presumption. Let me walk in faith according to Your Word.

SQUASH GREED, REID

"Again, the devil taketh him up into an exceeding high mountain, and sheweth him all the kingdoms of the world, and the glory of them; And saith unto him, All these things will I give thee, if thou wilt fall down and worship me."
Matthew 4:8-9

Here we see the devil tempt Jesus with the kingdoms of the world. Imagine how attractive he must have made this offer—the beautiful gardens, picturesque works of stone, stately mansions, breathtaking palaces, magnificent temples, towering buildings and enormous land mass. However, Jesus turned it down. I believe it was for three reasons: (1) He is God; (2) It wasn't the devil's to offer; and (3) He would eventually get it. A person controlled by a spirit of greed would likely have taken Satan up on his offer.

Greed is a selfish and excessive desire to acquire more than one needs and being controlled by that desire. There are three causes of greed and they begin with the letter D. *Dread*—the fear I might lose everything so I better get all I can. *Desire*—a craving to have more than actually needed. *Delight*—the desire to experience the

17

delights of pleasure and the more things obtained, the more pleasure one receives. In 1 Timothy 6:6-18, Paul gives Timothy three principles for overcoming greed. First, be content with what you have. "But godliness with contentment is great gain. For we brought nothing into this world, and it is certain we can carry nothing out. And having food and raiment let us be therewith content" (6-8). Second, trust God not riches. "Charge them that are rich in this world, that they be not high-minded, nor trust in uncertain riches, but in the living God, who giveth us richly all things to enjoy" (17). Third, exercise generosity. "That they do good, that they be rich in good works, ready to distribute, willing to communicate" (18). Pay attention to these three principles to squash greed, Reid.

Greed is expensive. It can cost you peace of mind, family and friends.

Prayer

Dear Jehovah Jireh, You are the God who meets all of our needs. I thank You because all I have needed Your hand hath provided. Please cleanse me of any spirit of covetous and greed and let me be a faithful steward of the things You have blessed me with.

GUARD YOUR WORSHIP, CHIP

*"Then saith Jesus unto him, Get thee hence, Satan: for it is written, Thou shalt worship the Lord thy God, and him only shalt thou serve."*Matthew 4:10

The third temptation presented to Jesus by the devil was in the area of worship. He took Jesus up into a high mountain and showed him all the kingdoms of the world and their glory. Then he told Jesus, "All these things will I give thee, if thou wilt fall down and worship me" (9). When the devil made this offer to Jesus, one thing he failed to realize was that Jesus already had the legal right to possess them. So Satan was offering Jesus something He already owned. But notice when Jesus rebuked the devil, He didn't say, "How can you give me something I already own?" No, Jesus was more concerned about protecting His worship. He loved the Father so much that He could not fathom worshipping anyone but the Lord God.

Even though the devil has a group of people who worship him today, he is not content with this. He also wants the worship of God's people but he knows they will not outright worship him. Therefore he entices them to worship him in subtle ways. He gets them to bow before the god of materialism. He gets them to bow before the god of self-indulgence. He gets them to bow before the god of amusement. He gets them to bow before the god of self and ego. God's people must take a page out of the playbook of Jesus and guard your worship, Chip.

A preacher once said, many Christians worship the false deity Baal—foot-baal, basket-baal and base-baal.

Prayer

Heavenly Father, don't let me be tricked into worshipping a false deity, but let me reserve my worship for You and You alone.

HAVE A JOYFUL DAY, TAY

*"When any one heareth the word of the kingdom, and understandeth it not, then cometh the wicked one, and catcheth away that which was sown in his heart. This is he which received seed by the way side."*Matthew 13:19

This verse is a part of the Parable of the Sower and the Soils. It describes a sower who goes forth to sow seed, some of which fell on bad soil and some fell into good ground. The ones that fell on bad soil died but the ones falling into the good soil brought forth fruit. The seed which fell by the wayside, described in verse 19 above, has always caused me great concern. The fact that the wicked one, who is the devil, can snatch the seed (the Word of God) out of the heart of an individual is very troubling.

Satan not only tries to steal the Word out of people's hearts, he also tries to take the joy out of their hearts. There are times in life when we deal with setbacks. It can be a disagreement with our spouse, a sewer backing up into the house, a washing machine breaking down or problems with a vehicle. The devil will work through these things to frustrate us, discourage us and steal our

21

joy. When we find ourselves depleted of joy, we should stop by God's filling stations. The first filling station is the presence of God. In Psalm 16:11 we read, "In thy presence is fullness of joy." We experience the joy of His presence by worshipping Him in song, bowing before Him in prayer or just being still and knowing He is God (Ps. 46:10). Another filling station is the Word of God. Psalm 19:8 says, "The statutes of the Lord are right, rejoicing the heart." Reading how Biblical characters held on to their joy in the midst of calamity can be a great source of encouragement. When we do these things, no matter what comes our way, we can have a joyful day, Ta!

This joy that we have, the devil did not give it to us and we should not let him take it away.

Prayer

I thank You, Most Gracious Lord, for the gift of joy. I understand that my joy is not based on my circumstances but on You. Please help me to remember this and be joyful in whatever I may be going through.

FOLLOW THE EXAMPLE OF NEHEMIAH, JEREMIAH

*"The enemy that sowed them is the devil;
the harvest is the end of the world;
and the reapers are the angels."*
Matthew 13:39

After the Babylonia captivity, many of the Jewish people went back to the homeland in Jerusalem. One Old Testament character by the name of Nehemiah received word from some of the returnees that the wall around the city was still in ruins (Neh. 1:1-3). His heart was so burdened that he returned and headed up an effort to restore the wall. With great excitement he began the project but it was met with great opposition. He faced ridicule (4:1-3), opposition by the enemy (4:10-17), internal conflict (5:1-5), and wolves in sheep's clothing (6:1-4). Despite all this, he completed rebuilding the wall in fifty-two days (6:15-19). He was able to manage the project and not get discouraged.

The devil is the master of discouragement; he tries to discourage God's people primarily through opposition. In Matthew 13:39, he is identified as "the enemy" which points to his work of opposing God and His servants. As believers we can overcome discouragement from the devil by having a spirit of Jeremiah which is:

- A Spirit of Prayer (4:4-5, 9a).
- A Spirit of Determination (4:6).
- A Spirit of Awareness (9).
- A Spirit of Courage (14).
- A Spirit of Trust (14b-15a, 20).
- A Spirit of Wisdom (16-18, 21).
- A Spirit of Perseverance (Neh. 6:1-4).

"One of the devil's biggest tools in the life of the believer is discouragement."
Author Unknown

Prayer

"Father, there will be times when the enemy takes away my enthusiasm, spirit and courage. When this happens, please help me identify the cause of my discouragement and realize what it is doing to me. Help me overcome discouragement by having the spirit of Nehemiah.

DISCONNECT FROM THE SCREEN, DEAN

"But he turned, and said unto Peter, Get thee behind me, Satan: thou art an offence unto me: for thou savourest not the things that be of God, but those that be of men." Matthew 16:23

Near the end of Jesus' life on earth, He began to discuss with the disciples His death and resurrection. The Apostle Peter struggled with the concept of Jesus' death, and Matthew records the following words. "*Then Peter took him, and began to rebuke him, saying, Be it far from thee, Lord: this shall not be unto thee*" (Matt. 16:22). Jesus was on a mission to seek and save the lost. The only way this was going to be done was by His death on the cross. Satan was working through Peter to distract Christ from finishing the work He came to do. Jesus, staying focused on His mission and realizing that Satan was behind Peter's words, said, "Get thee behind me, Satan." The devil is the master of distractions, but Jesus was not going to let the devil distract Him.

We live in a society with many screens—computers, tablets, smart phones, gaming devices, televisions, etc. The devil is using these things to distract people from that which is meaningful. Parents and children are so busy looking at screens, they do not have time for family togetherness. Husbands and wives have their faces in screens so much they don't have time to work on their relationships. As much of a blessing as technology is, the devil has used it to be the source of distractions that take people away from significant things in life. On one occasion, Jesus went to the house of Mary and Martha. Mary sat focused at the feet of Jesus while Martha was distracted by other things. Jesus said to Martha that Mary was not distracted but "hath chosen that good part, which shall not be taken away from her." One way to choose that which is important is to disconnect from the screen, Dean.

Electronic devices only last for a certain period of time but relationships last for a lifetime.

Prayer

Lord, let me be sensitive to know when to disconnect from the screen and connect with others.

YOU HAVE TO PRAY DAILY, BAILEY

"And the Lord said, Simon, Simon, behold, Satan hath desired to have you, that he may sift you as wheat: But I have prayed for thee, that thy faith fail not."
Luke 22:31-32

In Biblical times, after the wheat was ground up it was placed on a sieve. The farmer would then rapidly shake it back and forth until the wheat fell through and the chaff remained on the sieve. The chaff would then be thrown in the air and be blown away by the wind. Jesus informed Peter and the rest of the disciples (the "you" is plural) that the devil wanted to violently shake their lives. Satan is on a mission to seek and destroy the disciples of Christ, but praise God, Jesus said, "I have prayed for thee."

Jesus not only realized the disciples were in a spiritual battle, He was also led to do something about it—He prayed for them. He did not just offer up a quickie prayer but His prayer was from the heart and specific. First, the word "prayed" comes from the Greek term *deomia* and it means "to plead or beg." This prayer was not some fly-by-night prayer but one in which

27

He was making an emotional appeal from the recesses of His heart. Second, Jesus also prayed a specific prayer of deliverance for them, that when they came under Satan's attack their faith would not fail. He did not pray some general prayer but a specific prayer related to their warfare. Jesus knows the enemy. He knows his wiles and schemes. He knew exactly how Satan was going to come at His disciples. So His prayer was not vague, it was targeted and pinpointed.

As believers we are in a daily battle with the devil and one of the ways we can resist him is to pray daily, Bailey. Taking a page from the battle plans of Jesus, these prayers should be from the heart and specific.

The devil stands against us daily, therefore we should kneel against him daily.

Prayer

Father, help me to rise up against the devil every day in prayer.

DON'T BE LUSTY, RUSTY

"Ye are of your father the devil, and the lusts of your father ye will do." John 8:44

This statement is a result of Jesus being in an intense dialogue with the religious leaders of His day. They were hypocrites who claimed to have the patriarch Abraham as their father. Responding to their claim, Jesus let them know if Abraham was their father, they would do the works that Abraham did. Then He hit them with a stunning bit of information, He informed them they did the works of their father, except it was not Abraham but the devil. One of the works they inherited from their father the devil was lust. The word "lust" (Greek *epithumos*) refers to evil desires and passions.

Satan is the father of lust. Whenever a believer gives into the lusts of the flesh, he is not reflecting the character of God the Father, but the devil. This is why we should not allow lust to dwell in our hearts. Lust can come into our hearts in many shapes and forms—greed, gluttony, sexual immorality, jealousy, slothfulness, pleasure, alcohol and drugs. In order to have victory over lust, we must first give our lustful thoughts over to the Lord and ask Him for strength to overcome them. Second, we should not put ourselves in positions where lust in our lives is being fed. In doing this, we will not be lusty, Rusty.

Don't obey the lusts of the devil but the desires of the Lord.

Prayer

Dear God, give me strength to keep my heart pure so that my desires might be holy.

DON'T BE A FOOL, JEWEL

"And after the sop Satan entered into him [Judas]. Then said Jesus unto him, That thou doest, do quickly." John 13:27

Looking back just about everyone who has ever lived since the time of Christ knows that Judas was the one who betrayed Him. At the Last Supper he broke bread with Jesus and when Judas took the sop [*a piece of bread that was dipped into the cup*] the Bible says, "Satan entered into him." What is so amazing about Judas' betrayal is that he saw the power of Jesus displayed on a daily basis for almost three years. He saw the blind receive their sight, the lame healed and even the dead raised to life. How foolish it was of him to betray Christ. It is unbelievable that Judas would think that he could sell out Christ and get away with it. He was a fool to open himself up to be used by Satan.

If we are not careful, the devil can lead us to do some foolish things. We have seen Christians who have been blessed by the Lord who stop giving to Him when times get tough. We have seen believers flirt with a person of the opposite sex and end up having an affair. We have seen the children of God cheat on their income taxes and get in trouble with the IRS. We have seen those who claim Jesus as their personal Lord and Savior put God to the test by being presumptuous and calling it faith. Solomon said, "*The way of a fool is right in his own eyes: but he that hearkeneth unto counsel is wise*" (Prov. 12:15). A fool is a ripe candidate to be influenced by Satan, but the person who listens to wise counsel will not be a fool, Jewel.

A wise man sees the influence of Satan and learns from it, but the fool gives in to Satan's influence and is burned by it.

Prayer

Lord, give me a desire to seek for wisdom as silver, and a heart to search for it like a buried treasure.

KEEP YOUR LIFE CLEAN, GENE

*"Hereafter I will not talk much with you: for the prince of this world cometh, and hath nothing in me."*John 14:30

In John 14 Jesus was spending some precious time with His disciples before He went back to Heaven. He informed them that He was going to prepare a place for them (1-6) and He assured them that when He left the Holy Spirit would come to comfort them (15-26). In verse 30 He lets them know that He would not be spending much more time teaching them because Satan was going to work through Judas and He would be betrayed. He called Satan "the prince of this world" but more striking He said that he, "hath nothing in me." Wow! The devil was coming to deliver a blow of condemnation against Jesus, but when he threw the punch there would be nothing for him to hit. Jesus is sinless and when the devil tried to condemn Him there was no basis for any accusation against Him. He was not able to find anything to latch on to.

As believers we cannot be sinless like Jesus, but we can be blameless. The word blameless is used several times in the New Testament and it

33

can mean "without a handle." The term was used to indicate that there is nothing to grab a hold of. For instance, if a person were to come to a door without a doorknob, there would be nothing to grab to open the door. When a believer lives a blameless life that means when Satan comes to grab a hold of some sin there is nothing for him to take hold of. This is why you should keep your life clean, Gene, in your character, conduct and conversation.

When the devil comes to the door of your heart, make sure there is no doorknob of sin for him to grab.

Prayer

Father, help me to read and pray, walk in the narrow way; help me to keep my life clean every day.

JUST TELL THE TRUTH, RUTH

*"But Peter said, Ananias, why hath
Satan filled thine heart to lie to
the Holy Ghost."* Acts 5:3

In the early church they practiced
something called "Commonism." No, I did not
say Communism. Commonism is where the
people willingly sold particular possessions and
shared them with other believers who were in
need (Acts 2:44-45; 4:32). The Lord blessed a
couple named Ananias and Sapphira to sell a
certain possession. But before they brought it
to the Apostles, they agreed to keep a certain
portion for themselves and lie about how much
it was sold for. When the husband turned in the
money, he lied to the disciples about how much
they received when it was sold. Notice who was
at the heart of their deception: Peter said, "Why
hath Satan filled thine heart to lie..." Because
they listened to Satan, both the husband and
wife lost their lives.

It is interesting that there are two key
passages in the Bible about lying. First it made
the Big Ten, *"Thou shalt not bear false witness
against thy neighbor"* (Ex. 20:16). Second, it

made the list of things that God hates. "*These six things doth the Lord hate: yea, seven are an abomination unto him: A proud look, a lying tongue, and hands that shed innocent blood. An heart that deviseth wicked imaginations, feet that be swift in running to mischief, A false witness that speaketh lies, and he that soweth discord among brethren*" (Prov. 6:16-19). To avoid committing a sin in the Big Ten or doing something that God hates, just tell the truth, Ruth.

Tell the truth and you will never have to remember what you said.

Prayer

O Lord, set a watch over my mouth to keep it from lying, and keep the door of my lips and let them only speak the truth.

DON'T LET SATAN TAKE YOUR PEACE, REESE

"And the God of peace shall bruise Satan under your feet shortly. The grace of our Lord Jesus Christ be with you. Amen."
Romans 16:20

Satan had crept into the Church of Rome in the form of false teachers. Paul is writing to believers there warning them to stay away from these purveyors of false doctrine. Then he writes a word of encouragement when he says that God would crush Satan under their feet. It is important to notice that God is referred to as the "God of peace." In spite of the work of Satan, they could take comfort that the God of peace had things under control and one day He would give them the ultimate victory over Satan.

Satan wants to disrupt our peace. However, we can stand against him in confidence knowing we have the peace of God and peace with God. Furthermore, we can rest with a calm spirit knowing that Satan cannot touch our lives unless the God of peace permits it. Even then it is under the watchful eye of God Almighty, so don't let him take your peace, Reese. In Psalm 23:2 the

God of Peace is compared to a shepherd who leads us "beside the still waters." The shepherd leads sheep to a lake or pond and not a river. The sheep cannot drink from a river because the turbulence will cause water to splash in its face, so the shepherd leads to still waters. The God of peace not only leads us to peaceful waters, He also forces Satan to watch us drink in peace.

No God, no peace.
Know God, know peace.

Prayer

Dear Jehovah Shalom, You are the God of peace! I realize Satan will attack me with a whole array of problems to disrupt my peace. Please let me have the blessed assurance that the God of peace is with me, and knowing this—let it be well with my soul.

YOU MUST REPENT, KENT

*"To deliver such an one unto Satan for the destruction of the flesh, that the spirit may be saved in the day of the Lord Jesus."*1 Corinthians 5:5

In the Corinthian church there was a man who was living in an immoral relationship. He was having sex with his stepmother (5:1). This sin was commonly known throughout the congregation but the leaders did not deal with it. Paul writes to them instructing them to put this man out of the church. He then makes an eye-opening statement, "deliver such an one unto Satan for the destruction of the flesh." When a believer is handed over to Satan it is solely for the sake of repentance. By giving Satan authority in the man's life, he could do to this man what he did to Job, take his possessions and health. The suffering this man was about to go through was God's way of chastising him, in order to get him to repent. Notice that the man is still saved.

Is there a sin in your life that you need to deal with before the Lord? Why not repent of it in order to avoid a time of suffering at the hand of Satan? In order to repent there are three things

39

you must do. The first is to confess it. In Psalm 51, when David wanted to repent, he confessed his sin to God. He accepted responsibility for it (3a), he did not try to sweep it under the rug (3b) and he identified the problem (5). The second thing he did was ask God to forgive him. He appealed to God's mercy and loving kindness for forgiveness. Twice he asked the Lord to blot out his transgressions/iniquities (1, 9). The third thing that David did was turn away from the wrong thing to do the right thing (13). When you confess your sin, ask for forgiveness for your sin and forsake your sin—that is what it means to repent, Kent.

Repent now and don't be turned over to Satan for the destruction of the flesh.

Prayer

Dear Father, "I acknowledge my sin unto thee, and mine iniquity have I not hid. I said, I will confess my transgressions unto the Lord; and thou forgavest the iniquity of my sin" (Ps. 32:5).

DISCIPLINE YOUR SEX, REX

"Defraud ye not one the other, except it be with consent for a time, that ye may give yourselves to fasting and prayer; and come together again, that Satan tempt you not for your incontinency."
1 Corinthians 7:5

There may be times when a married couple feels led to spend some devoted time in prayer and fasting. This may also be accompanied by abstinence from sexual activities. Paul's advice for this couple is when that time is over to immediately resume their sex life so that Satan cannot come in and tempt either individual to become sexually unfaithful. The word "incontinency" means lack of self-control or self-restraint. The devil knows this can be a time when the couple is sexually vulnerable. If they lack self-control he can quickly step in and use abstinence as a device to wreak havoc in a marriage.

Satan is the author of all types of sexual perversions. His objective is to find a weakness in a person's life and prey on it. He will do this with temptations that appeal to the lust of the flesh and the lust of the eyes. Where there is a lack of sexual integrity, the devil will seduce his victims with pornography, fornication, adultery and a whole array of immoral temptations. This is why we are told in 1 Thessalonians 4:3, *"For this is the will of God, even your sanctification, that ye should abstain from fornication [sexual sins]."* Believers should do their best to live holy lives and avoid immorality at all costs—to do this is to discipline your sex, Rex.

God designed sex to be a beautiful act between a husband and wife. Satan perverted it into an act of defilement and destruction in the lives of individuals.

Prayer

Gracious Father, teach me how to control my sexual desires and express them in healthy ways that honor You.

YOU HAVE TO FORGIVE, LIV

"To whom ye forgive any thing, I forgive also: for if I forgave any thing, to whom I forgave it, for your sakes forgave I it in the person of Christ; Lest Satan should get an advantage of us: for we are not ignorant of his devices."
2 Corinthians 2:10-11

In Paul's first letter to the Corinthian church, he identified a man living in a sexually immoral relationship. He reprimanded the leaders for their failure to deal with the situation and exhorted them to put this man out of the church (1 Cor. 5:1-5). Somewhere along the line this man got his heart right with the Lord and repented of his sin. Even though the man made things right with God, the church refused to forgive him and let him back into the fellowship. Paul admonishes the church in his second letter to forgive the man and restore him to the fellowship because failure to do so would give Satan an advantage over them.

The devil uses unforgiveness to wreak havoc in the lives of Christians. When we refuse to forgive, we open up our lives to be tormented by demons (Matt. 18:23-35). When we refuse to forgive, answers to our prayers are blocked (Mk. 11:24-26). When we refuse to forgive, we hinder our forgiveness from God (Matt. 6:15). When we refuse to forgive, it defiles our lives (Heb. 12:15). Forgiveness is to walk in the steps of our Father God. William Arthur Ward, in his book, *Thoughts of a Christian Optimist*, wrote: "We are most like beasts when we kill. We are most like men when we judge. We are most like God when we forgive." And might I add, "We are most like Satan when we don't forgive." Forgiveness is when we open the cage of our souls and release the resentment and ill will against the one who offended us. This is why you have to forgive, Liv.

It has been said, "Holding unforgiveness against someone is like drinking poison in the hope the other person gets sick."

Prayer

God, You are a forgiving God. In obedience to Your Word, help me forgive those who have offended me. By the power of the love you have put in me, let me follow Christ's example and forgive those who seek my harm.

DON'T BE UNAWARE, JAVIER

"Lest Satan should get an advantage of us: for we are not ignorant of his devices."
2 Corinthians 2:11

In the passage above, Paul is writing to the church in Corinth to get them to forgive a repentant brother. Their failure to forgive him leaves an open door for Satan to come in and tear the church apart. Paul says they should not let Satan get the upper hand by being ignorant of his devices. The word "devices" comes from the Greek word *noamata*, which makes reference to the mind. Satan has a lot of mind games or tricks that he tries to use on people. I heard a preacher say, "The devil has more tricks than a dog has fleas."

Paul said that we should not be "ignorant of his devices." The believer should be aware of the tricks of the devil. He is constantly laying traps for people to fall in. As we read the Word of God and are led by the Spirit of God, however, we become more and more aware of his schemes. On several occasions the Apostle said, "I would not have you to be ignorant brethren." Someone has jokingly said, "One of the fastest growing denominations in America today is that of the Ignorant Brethren." We can resist the devil by not being unaware, Javier.

If the devil tricks me once, shame on him; if he tricks me twice, shame on me.

Prayer

Dear Omniscient Father, don't let Satan get an advantage over me because of my ignorance. Give me wisdom to know and recognize his ploys and deceptions.

YOU MUST BE BORN AGAIN, KEN

"But if our gospel be hid, it is hid to them that are lost: In whom the god of this world hath blinded the minds of them which believe not, lest the light of the glorious gospel of Christ, who is the image of God, should shine unto them."
2 Corinthians 4:3-4

These verses let us know we should not underestimate the power of Satan. His sway over an unsaved person is so powerful that he can blind their minds to the light of the Gospel. It is difficult for unbelievers to clearly see the Gospel and it is further exacerbated by the god of this world. He is able to develop systems that contribute to the blinding process, even plunging sinners into greater depths of debauchery. He uses blinders of human and demonic philosophies to keep people from seeing the glorious Gospel of Christ.

The only way for these blinders to be removed is by a person coming to salvation through Jesus Christ. John, the beloved disciple wrote, *"He that committeth sin is of the devil; for the devil sinneth from the beginning. For this purpose the Son of God was manifested, that he* might destroy the works of the devil" (1 Jn. 3:8). Jesus Christ came to take the blinders off the eyes of unbelievers by destroying the works of the devil. A person can resist the devil and have victory over him, but you have to be born again, Ken.

The Christmas hymn "God Rest Ye Merry Gentlemen" contains three powerful lines that are apropos to this lesson: *God rest ye merry gentlemen, let nothing you dismay. Remember Christ, our savior was born on Christmas Day. To save us all from Satan's power when we were gone astray.*

Prayer

Father, I pray for my unsaved loved ones. I ask that You would allow the Holy Spirit to shine the light of the Gospel upon them and they would receive it.

DON'T BE FOOLED BY THE LIGHT, DWIGHT

"And no marvel; for Satan himself is transformed into an angel of light."
2 Corinthians 11:14

In this passage Paul is issuing a warning concerning false prophets who were promoting a doctrine that was very alluring and appealing. They packaged it in wrappings that were very attractive. Paul compares them to Satan by saying that we should not be surprised because he can transform himself "into an angel of light."

The devil is not walking around dressed in a red suit, with pointed ears, a tail and carrying a pitchfork. He presents himself as an angel of light, this is an indication of his ability to deceive. An angel of light would be one who looks beautiful and truthful. This is the way he presents himself outwardly, yet inwardly he is filled with lies and deceit.

Believers must be able to recognize and stay away from this angel of light. He comes in the form of appealing relationships, desired material possessions, great sounding doctrinal philosophies and attractive temptations. This light can be recognized when one personally studies the truths found in the Word of God, sits under sound Bible teaching and is sensitive to the leading of the Holy Spirit. In doing this, a person can avoid the deceptive light, Dwight.

Just like all that glitters is not gold, all angels are not angels of light.

Prayer

Dear All-Knowing Father, I pray that you would give me discernment to distinguish light from darkness, truth from error, right from wrong, pure from impure and moral from immoral.

PUT HIM UNDER YOUR FEET, PETE

"And hath put all things under his feet."
Ephesians 1:22

What a powerful word picture this is! Christ has put all things under His feet. The imagery comes from the ancient world where a king would put his foot on the neck of his conquered enemy. This act symbolized that the enemy was in total subjection to the king. In the previous verse (21) some of the things under Christ's feet are listed—principality, power, might and dominion. These words refer to Satan and his demonic forces. Praise God! Jesus has put his foot on the neck of the devil and all he represents.

Later in the Book of Ephesians, Paul would say the believer has been raised up together, and made to sit together in heavenly places in Christ Jesus (Eph. 2:6). It only stands to reason, if we are seated together with Christ in heavenly places and He has all things under His feet, we have the same authority. You can put the devil under your feet, Pete— realizing your position in Christ and walking in authority over the evil one. I heard a Christian rapper say in a song:

"You don't have to work with the shovel, you've got the power to step on the devil."

Prayer

Exalted Savior, please remind me that when I feel overwhelmed by the devil, You have given me the authority over him. Even though he has power, I serve the One who has all power and is able to subdue the forces of darkness.

TRUST AND OBEY, RAY

*"Wherein in time past ye walked according to the course of this world, according to the prince of the power of the air, the spirit that now worketh in the children of disobedience."*Ephesians 2:2

In this verse Satan is identified as the "prince of the power of the air." This phrase indicates that he has authority in heavenly places and is able to work in the lives of the unsaved. There was a time as unbelievers that we were dead in sin but now we have been given spiritual life. As unbelievers, we were children of disobedience under the authority of Satan.

As you read this brief devotion, is there an area of your life in which you are living in disobedience to God? This is a characteristic of one who is walking according to the prince of the power of the air. Peter said we have been given *"exceeding great and precious promises: that by these ye might be partakers of the divine nature, having escaped the corruption that is in the world through lust"* (2 Pet. 1:4). We are partakers of the divine nature; that means we have God's nature living in us in the person of the Holy Spirit. We are not God but we have his nature in us. This gives us the power to obey the things the Lord has spoken to us in His Word and through His Spirit. We don't have to live anymore as children of disobedience under the prince of the power of the air, we can trust and obey, Ray.

Are you in obedience to the Prince of Peace or the prince of the power of the air?

Prayer

Lord, let me sit at Your feet, in fellowship sweet; and have a mind always to do Your good will.

GIVE THE DEVIL NO PLACE, GRACE

"Neither give place to the devil."
Ephesians 4:27

In this verse, Paul instructs the believer to not "give place to the devil." The NIV translates the phrase "neither give place to the devil" as "do not give the devil a foothold." The word foothold is a military term and it was used to describe a beachhead. This is where the invading army comes onto the shore of its enemy and occupies a small area. The beachhead establishes a basis for the invading army to bring in more military power to move out and launch a full-scale attack against its enemy.

Paul is letting us know that if we give the devil a crack, he will use it to establish a place to launch an attack on us. In Proverbs 4:23 we are told to diligently guard our hearts. This means we are to be on the lookout for any places where the devil can come and establish a foothold. We should be on the watch for any emotional problem, material possession, relationship issue or spiritual sin that would give the devil an opportunity to unleash an attack on us. This is why we need to give the devil no place, Grace.

When you seal up the crack, you break the devil's back.

Prayer

Father, give me an awareness of any breaches in my life that would be an open door for Satan to work.

BE NICE, BRYCE

*"Neither give place to the devil" "And be
ye kind one to another, tenderhearted,
forgiving one another, even as God
for Christ's sake hath forgiven you."*
Ephesians 4:27, 32

In verse 27, Paul says that we should not give place [a foothold] to the devil. Then he goes on to list the things that give him a foothold—stealing (28), corrupt communication (29) grieving the Holy Spirit (30), bitterness, wrath, anger, clamour, evil speaking, and malice (31). In verse 32, Paul lists the antidote to these evil words and actions—"be ye kind one to another, tender-hearted."

The devil loves tearing up churches and he uses individuals to do it. In Galatians 5:15 (NIV), Paul gives the following warning to members in the church, *"If you bite and devour each other, watch out or you will be destroyed by each other."* The word devour means "to eat." Someone has said when one human being eats another, it is cannibalism. Paul is warning believers against becoming spiritual cannibals through gossip, backbiting, criticism and evil actions.

The antidote for spiritual cannibalism or "devouring one another" is kindness. The word "kindness" comes from the Greek word *philadephos*, which means "brotherly love." This is where we get the name for the city of Philadelphia, "the city of brotherly love." We should treat others in the body of Christ with brotherly love. This means we handle each other with gentleness and respect, dwell together in unity, work out our problems in love, and serve one another. When we do this, we are being nice, Bryce.

The Lord commands His blessing to fall upon those who are treating each other with brotherly love.

Prayer

Dear God, help me to add patience to godliness; and to godliness brotherly kindness; and to brotherly kindness love (2 Pet. 1:6-7).

DON'T BE SO BUSY, LIZZY

"Put on the whole armour of God, that ye may be able to stand against the wiles of the devil." Ephesians 6:11

Paul said to put on the whole armor of God to stand against the wiles of the devil. The word "wiles" comes from the Greek word *methodia* and means schemes or tricks. This word was used of a ferocious animal in the wild that followed its prey unaware and attacked it at an opportune moment. Notice that the King James Version translates the word in the plural "wiles." The devil has more wiles or tricks than a pharmacy has pills.

One of the devil's great tools is busyness. I heard the story about a convention that Satan held for his demons. In his opening remarks he said, "I have come up with a new strategy in the war against Christians." "What is it?" queried one of the demons. Satan replied with delight, "We can't stop them from attending church, reading their Bibles, praying or spending time with their families. But we can distract them by keeping them busy. If we keep them busy with insignificant things, they will not have time for

the important things God wants them to do."
Dear Christian, have you fallen for this trick of
the devil? Get your priorities right and don't be
so busy, Lizzy.

Someone has astutely said, "The word busy is an acronym for *Being Under Satan's Yoke.*"

Prayer

Dear Heavenly Father, help me to take stock
of my life day by day. Please convict my heart
if I have become too busy to spend time on the
things that are important. Give me wisdom to
do this so that I will not be under Satan's yoke.

WATCH OUT FOR
THE TRIVIA,
ALYVIA

*"Put on the whole armour of God, that ye may
be able to stand against the wiles of the devil."*
Ephesians 6:11

One of the meanings of the word trivia is
"things that are unimportant, irrelevant, trivial
or unnecessary." According to the verse above,
the devil has many "wiles" (Greek *methodia*),
schemes, scams, deceptions, and tricks, one of
which is getting God's people to focus on that
which is unimportant.

The story is told of a man who was making
his schedule out for the week. His plan included
starting everyday by reading the morning
newspaper and after that spending the majority of
his day on the job. When he got home from work,
his plans included housework and preparing for
work the next day. His weekends included pretty
much the same thing only he substituted playing
video games and other recreational activities for
the hours spent at work during the week. This
man, like many today, made no time for the
important things of life such as devoting time to
God in prayer and Bible reading, spending time

with his family and serving the Lord. In order to keep from falling into the hole that man fell into, watch out for the trivia, Alyvia.

Don't fill the container of your life with sand (unimportant things) and not have room for the rocks (important things).

Prayer

Father please give me the wisdom to know how to prioritize my time according to Your will. My desire is to pray the prayer of Jesus in John 17:4, *"I have finished the work which thou gavest me to do."*

COMPREHEND: YOU CAN'T SEE HIM, JIM

*"For we wrestle not against flesh and blood."*Ephesians 6:12

In this verse Paul is informing us that we are in a battle against an invisible enemy. Even though these attacks seem to come through people and circumstances, the battle really isn't against flesh and blood. It is against Satan and his host of unseen fallen angels.

Often when we are under attack, we respond by launching a counterattack against a flesh and blood foe—our spouses, co-workers, neighbors, etc. When we do this, we are fighting the battle on the wrong level. We have to get off this earthly level and fight this enemy on the battlefield of the heavenly realms. By doing thi,s we engage our opponents with spiritual artillery.

God has equipped His people for this battle with specific weapons of warfare. These weapons are the Bible (Matt. 4:1-11), the armor of God (Eph. 6:10-18), the name of Jesus (Acts 16:18), the blood of Jesus (Rev. 12:11), fasting (Matt. 17:14-21), and praise (2 Chron. 20:21). We need these weapons to fight the battle because we can't see him, Jim.

You cannot fight an invisible enemy with fleshly weapons.

Prayer

Father, show me how to properly fight against an enemy that I cannot see.

BE SINCERE, EMIR

"Put on the whole armour of God, that ye may be able to stand against the wiles of the devil." Ephesians 6:11

"Stand therefore, having your loins girt about with truth." Ephesians 6:14

The loins of the Roman soldier were covered with a leather belt which was more like an apron. It held the soldiers garment together and served as a place on which to hang his armor. Paul tells the believer to put on the belt of truth. From the beginning Satan has attacked the truth of God (Gen. 3:1ff.), and he continues to do so until this present day. Jesus said he *"is a liar, and the father of lies"* (John 8:44). He also aims for chinks in the armor of believers. When Christians lie, are deceitful or involved in all types of hypocrisy, they open the door for Satan to come in and do his dirt. For this reason, Paul instructs the believer to be "girded with the truth."

One way to be girded with the truth is to live a life of integrity. In Psalm 26:1, the psalmist cries out, *"Judge me, O Lord; for I have walked in mine integrity."* In this verse the plea is for

God to look at his situation and fight his cause because he was living a blameless life. The word "integrity" (Heb. *tome)* comes from a related Hebrew word found in Leviticus 1:3, which refers to an animal sacrifice and is translated "without blemish." Whereas a blemished sacrifice was tainted and deemed unacceptable, a sacrifice without blemish was suitable to offer. Therefore, integrity can be defined as being without blemish in conscience, character and conduct. When Satan hurls an accusation at the believer, if he is living a life of integrity, it will not stick because he is being sincere, Emir.

Are you one thing in public and another in private? Who you are in private is who you are.

Prayer

"Search me, O God, and know my heart: try me, and know my thoughts: And see if there be any wicked way in me, and lead me in the way everlasting." Psalm 139:23-24

STRIVE TO BE HOLY, FOLEY

"Put on the whole armour of God, that ye may be able to stand against the wiles of the devil." Ephesians 6:11

"...having on the breastplate of righteousness" Ephesians 6:14

The breastplate was a piece of armor that covered the full torso of the soldier. It was often made of leather or heavy linen, and many pieces of small metal were sewn on to it. The breastplate protected the heart, lungs, and upper body. The devil wants to attack God's people, especially in the area of righteousness. The breastplate of righteousness, which is holy living, provides protection from the enemy.

In 2 Corinthians 7:1, Paul says we are to perfect holiness. The word "perfect" comes from the Greek world *epiteleo* and it means "to bring to an end or completion." But this is not just any end or completion but to an ordained perfect end. In order for this to take place, the believer must practice holiness.

In 1 Tim. 4:7-8, Paul said, *"...exercise thyself rather unto godliness. For bodily exercise profiteth little: but godliness is profitable unto all things.*" The word "exercise" comes from a Greek word that is the origin for our English word *gymnasium*. In the culture of Paul's day, it was a term that represented rigorous training on the part of the athlete. They would often train in the nude to get the maximum results from their training. If ancient athletes went through all this for something that only "profits a little," how much more should the believer exercise unto godliness which is profitable in all things? Therefore, strive to be holy, Foley.

The best way to be holy is to practice every day.

Prayer

Dear God, help me to take time each and every day to spend time with You and when I leave Your presence, let me reflect Your character.

NO NEED TO WORRY, SURRY

"Put on the whole armour of God, that ye may be able to stand against the wiles of the devil." Ephesians 6:11

"…And your feet shod with the preparation of the gospel of peace." Ephesians 6:15

The Roman soldier wore a heavy-soled military shoe or sandal bound by thongs over the instep and around the ankle. The soles were thickly studded with metal or nails to ensure firm footing for travel and for fighting. The military sandal protected the soldier's feet and made it possible for him to move with quick and certain steps. One of Satan's objectives is to rob believers of their peace and cause them to worry. When our feet are shod with the preparation of the Gospel of Peace, we have two assurances. First, we have the assurance of stability in the battle. We have the promise of God that when we put on the sandals of the Gospel of Peace, we will be able to stand firm. Second, we have the assurance of shelter in the battle. Isaiah 54:17 says, *"No weapon that is formed against thee shall prosper."* The shoes give us peace that nothing can harm us because we are under God's protection.

In Matthew 6:25-34, Jesus gives us three principles to overcome Satan and worrying. First, there is the principle of control—you can control your worry. Twice in this passage Jesus says "Do not worry" (25a, 31). The fact that Jesus commanded people not to worry, demonstrates that it can be controlled. Second, there is the principle of Fatherhood. God is our Father and because of that there is no reason to worry. Our Father provides food and clothing (25b) and is taking care of creation (26, 28, 29, 30). He knows what we have need of (32) and takes care of us as we seek Him (33). Third, there is the principle of uselessness. Worry is useless because it cannot change today (27), and worry is useless because it cannot change tomorrow (34). Because of these three principles, there is no need to worry, Surry.

Corrie ten Boom said, "Worry does not empty tomorrow of its sorrow, it empties today of its strength."

Prayer

Dear Jehovah Shalom, though Satan attacks me from every side, I will not worry because I know that You are on the throne.

YOU HAVE TO BELIEVE, STEVE

"Put on the whole armour of God, that ye may be able to stand against the wiles of the devil." Ephesians 6:11

"Above all, taking the shield of faith, wherewith ye shall be able to quench all the fiery darts of the wicked." Ephesians 6:16

The shield spoken of here was made of wood and overlaid with metal. It was covered with linen or leather and soaked in water to absorb fiery arrows. It was about 2-1/2 feet wide and 4 feet long, and was designed to cover the whole body. The purpose of the Shield of Faith is to extinguish all the flaming arrows that Satan launches at the believer. The enemy cannot possess the believer, so he attacks him in other ways. He launches flaming missiles against him and they come quick and unexpected. In order to be able to quench and deflect the arrows of the enemy, we must take up the Shield of Faith.

In order to take a stand against the devil, we must be like Abraham and have a strong faith (Rom. 4:19-20). Notice the following characteristics of Abraham's faith:

1. Abraham believed when there was no hope: *"Who against hope believed in hope, that he*

might become the father of many nations, according to that which was spoken, So shall thy seed be" (Rom. 4:18).

2. Abraham believed without becoming weak in faith: "*And being not weak in faith…*" (Rom 4:19).

3. Abraham was not discouraged by his own limitations: "*…he considered not his own body now dead, when he was about an hundred years old, neither yet the deadness of Sarah's womb*" (Rom. 4:19).

4. Abraham put his faith in the promises of God: "*He staggered not at the promise of God*"(Rom. 4:20).

5. Abraham did not waver between belief and unbelief: "*He staggered not at the promise of God through unbelief; but was strong in faith, giving glory to God; And being fully persuaded that, what he had promised, he was able also to perform*"(Rom. 4:20-21).

To stand against the devil, you have to believe, Steve.

"He that cometh to God must believe that he is, and that he is a rewarder of them that

**_diligently seek him_"
(Hebrews 11:6).**

Prayer

Father, give me a faith that believes You can do exceeding and abundantly above all that I can ask or think.

BE ABLE TO DISCERN, VERN

"Put on the whole armour of God, that ye may be able to stand against the wiles of the devil." Ephesians 6:11

"And take the helmet of salvation." Ephesians 6:17

The Roman soldier had a bronze helmet with a leather strap on it. Some helmets were made of thick leather covered with metal plates and others of heavy molded or beaten metal. It was usually adorned with some figure. Most helmets had cheek pieces to protect the face and others had visors to protect the whole face.

From a spiritual standpoint, the helmet is needed to protect the mind. Satan can hit us in the head with deadly wounds. He can cause us to doubt the Word of God (Gen. 3:1), he can deceive us (2 Cor. 11:3-4), and he can get us to follow false doctrine (1 Tim. 4:1). The main feature of the helmet is discernment, which is divine enlightenment by the Holy Spirit to recognize whether a spirit or teaching is from God or Satan, is good or evil, or is genuine or a lie. Discernment is very important for believers today. The devil uses many voices in the world to speak to us. Many of these voices are false and deceptive. Exercising discernment enables us to know and follow the voice of truth.

It is reported that dogs were used in vast mansions and palaces to alert the residents to rats. When the dog got up and began to sniff throughout the building, it was said that he smelled a rat. This phrase caught on and is used whenever someone or something is suspicious. Discernment is the gift to be able to smell a rat—to tell whether a teaching is from God or from the devil (1 Tim. 4:1), to distinguish truth from error and right from wrong (1 John. 4:1-6), to tell the difference between the true Gospel of Christ and another gospel (Gal. 1:8-9), and to distinguish pure motives from impure motives (Acts 8:18-23).

The Bereans were discerning individuals; after listening to Paul, they searched the Scriptures to see if he was teaching the truth (see Acts 17:11). They were able to discern, Vern.

The devil is a rat and the only way to smell him is through the nose of discernment.

Prayer

Father, teach me to study Your Word and become so familiar with it that I will be able to discern the difference between right and wrong.

PICK UP THE SWORD, WARD

*"Put on the whole armour of God, that ye may be able to stand against the wiles of the devil."*Ephesians 6:11

*"...and the sword of the Spirit, which is the word of God"*Ephesians 6:17

The sword Paul refers to here is a *machaira*, the Greek word for sword. It varied in length from six to eighteen inches and was generally used in hand-to-hand combat. This type of sword was carried in a sheath and attached to the belt. It had to be ready to use in a moment's notice. The sword is both an offensive and defensive weapon. Defensively, it is able to block the strokes of the enemy's sword. When Satan attacks us, we can fend him off by believing and standing on the Word of God. Offensively, we can use the Word to put Satan on the run by quoting verses that instruct us to submit to God and resist the devil (James 4:7).

Why is it the Word doesn't work in the lives of Christians when they are attacked by the devil? The answer is simple. The Word of God is powerless when it is used apart from the rest of the armor. If you quote the Bible, but you don't live it, you will have no power. You can't walk around without the Breastplate of Righteousness lying, cheating, and scheming, and then expect that memorizing a verse is going to change your life. If you have no desire to live righteously, if you are knee deep in sin, the Word will have no power in your life. If you are walking around without the Helmet of Salvation carrying doubts about your own salvation, how can you trust God for the salvation of someone else? Satan knows the Word, but he doesn't have the armor. You can't have the Word without the rest of the armor. Satan has no integrity; he is "the father of lies." He has no righteousness, he is a murderer and the father of all sin. He is not "saved" and has no peace. The Word without integrity, holiness, peace, faith or the assurance of salvation is ineffective in the life of a believer. Pick up the Sword, Ward!

Understanding and properly using the Bible will keep Satan away from you or Satan will keep you away from the Bible.

Prayer

Dear Lord, please order my steps in Your Word and let Satan have no dominion over me.

DON'T LOOK FOR AN EXCUSE TO STALL, PAUL

*"Wherefore we would have come unto you, even I Paul, once and again; but Satan hindered us."*1 Thessalonians 2:18

During his three missionary journeys, God used the Apostle Paul to start many churches and one was in the city of Thessalonica. After establishing it and then moving on, sometime later he had a desire to return to the city to see how they were doing but Satan hindered him. The obstacle that hampered him may have been physical but the devil was behind it. Satan is in the business of getting God's people to delay doing things that need to be done—this is called procrastination.

Procrastination is one of the main tools of the devil. There are many reasons for procrastination— "I am not sure what to do"— that's uncertainty. "I am waiting for the right time"—that's making an excuse. "I am afraid"— that's fear. "I don't feel like doing it right now"— that's slothfulness. There are also several important spiritual matters people put off until a later time—"I'll give my life to Christ someday." "One day I will start to read my Bible and pray." "I'll take care of that sin tomorrow." "I will eventually get to that church project." Procrastination can be very harmful to self and others. Whenever we find ourselves procrastinating, we should overcome Satan by asking God for the strength and wisdom to do the things that must be done and not look for an excuse to stall, Paul.

"The best way to get something done is to begin."
Author Unknown

Prayer

Lord, please give me strength when I have a tendency to procrastinate. Give me the motivation to start what needs to be done, and the endurance to complete it.

LEARN NOT TO BLASPHEME, HAKIM

"Of whom is Hymenaeus and Alexander; whom I have delivered unto Satan, that they may learn not to blaspheme."
1 Timothy 1:20

Hymenaeus and Alexander were two false teachers in the early church. Paul told Timothy they should be put out of the church and delivered to Satan because they were blasphemers. Evidently these men were teaching some heretical things about God that were not true. The act of delivering them to Satan was moving them from under the protective umbrella of the church, to be open for Satan to have full access to work in their lives. The end result of their removal from God's protective hedge was, they would "learn not to blaspheme."

As children of God, we should avoid being delivered to Satan for discipline at all costs. In order to do this, we should seek to understand the truth about God found in His Word. Many people today are saying things about God that are not true. Some make Him out to be a genie in a bottle, just rub it and God will pop out and grant you whatever you want. Some make Him out to be a big policeman in the sky, waiting for someone to do wrong so He can cuff them and take them away to be punished. Some even paint a picture of God as accepting all types of wickedness and sin. Hymenaeus and Alexander were delivered to Satan because they were saying the wrong things about God. Let us read the Bible and find out the truth about Him and we will learn not to blaspheme, Hakim.

Do you eulogize God (say good and true things about Him), or blaspheme God (say bad and wrong things about Him)?

Prayer

Most Holy Father, let my lips praise you at all times and let my tongue only speak the truth about You.

BE FOR REAL, CAHLIL

"And Adam was not deceived, but the woman being deceived [by the serpent] was in the transgression." 1 Timothy 2:14

"And the great dragon was cast out, that old serpent, called the Devil, and Satan, which deceiveth the whole world: he was cast out into the earth, and his angels were cast out with him." Revelation 12:9

"And the devil that deceived them was cast into the lake of fire and brimstone, where the beast and the false prophet are, and shall be tormented day and night for ever and ever." Revelation 20:10

In the Scriptures listed above, we read that the devil is a deceiver. The Greek word for deceive is *planao*, which means "to mislead, misrepresent or deceive." The Merriam-Webster Dictionary defines the word deceive as "to cause to accept as true or valid what is false or invalid, to give a false impression."

Sometimes believers can deceive others, this is known as being a hypocrite. The word "hypocrite" comes from the Greek word *hypokrisis*. During New Testament times, it was used to refer to an actor on stage. These individuals would cover their faces with masks and pretend to be someone other than themselves. Many today say they are Christians but they are hypocrites because their lifestyles do not reflect who they claim to be. Let me offer the following advice to avoid being a hypocrite. First, be honest and truthful in what you say. Saying something other than the truth is to be a hypocrite. Second, live a life of righteousness, which means to do that which is right. To do otherwise is to be unrighteous and a hypocrite. Third, be a person of integrity. Don't say one thing in public and do something else in private.

Anyone who follows this advice is being for real, Cahlil.

One way to shame the devil is to be honest at all times.

Prayer

Dear Heavenly Father, help me to be real and genuine and let it be grounded in You—the One who is the truth.

STAY AWAY FROM THE OCCULT, WALT

"Now the Spirit speaketh expressly, that in the latter times some shall depart from the faith, giving heed to seducing spirits, and doctrines of devils."
1 Timothy 4:1

The Bible makes it clear that in the last days there will be a rise in curiosity and involvement with seducing spirits and doctrines of devils. In our society today, this shows up in the form of the occult. The word occult means that which is dark, mysterious and hidden. This is an area where Satan and his forces exercise great authority. The occult covers areas such as astrology, witchcraft, necromancy, séances, tarot cards, fortune telling, palm reading, clairvoyance, Ouija boards, magic, mind reading, and other such practices.

In the Old Testament, God said He would separate the soul involved in occultic practices from His people (Lev. 20:6). He knew that those involved in Satanic customs would influence others for evil, therefore He said, "cut them off." In the same way today, when people experiment with the occult, they are influenced by evil spirits. Even though a demon cannot possess a Christian, if he dabbles in dark things, a wicked spirit can attach itself to the believer's life. When this happens, the demon can have great influence, wreaking havoc in the life of the individual. Furthermore, God warned His people to stay as far away from these things as possible (Deut. 18:9-12). This is why you should stay away from the occult, Walt.

We should be so familiar with the light (God's Word) that we have no problem recognizing the darkness (the occult).

Prayer

Dear Father of Light, we know that people often get involved in the occult through innocence and inquisitiveness. Help us be aware of those seemingly harmless doors that swing open to the world of the occult.

DON'T BE AN IDLE LADY, SADIE

"And withal they learn to be idle, wandering about from house to house; and not only idle, but tattlers also and busybodies, speaking things which they ought not. I will therefore that the younger women marry, bear children, guide the house, give none occasion to the adversary to speak reproachfully. For some are already turned aside after Satan." 1 Timothy 5:13-15

In this chapter, Paul is addressing the care and responsibility of elderly and young widows. In speaking to the younger widows, he deals with the free time they have on their hands since their husbands have passed away. Instead of using that time to minister for the Lord, some had become idle and this led to them becoming gossips and busybodies. In addition, their idleness had led to something even more devastating, some had turned aside to follow Satan. Their inactivity had affected their commitment to Jesus Christ. Some had abandoned their dedication to the home and some had even remarried unbelievers—in essence they had turned aside after Satan.

Even though this passage is speaking specifically to younger widows, there is a message in it for all of us. Idleness and laziness go hand-in-hand, and the Book of Proverbs has a lot to say about this matter. They lead to hunger (Prov. 19:15), they cause one to waste resources (Prov. 18:9), they are at the foundation of making excuses (Prov. 22:13), and they result in destruction of property (Prov. 24:30-31). Instead of being idle, let us *"be ye stedfast, unmoveable, always abounding in the work of the Lord, forasmuch as ye know that your labour is not in vain in the Lord"* (1 Cor. 15:58). In doing this, you will not be an idle lady, Sadie.

If it has been said once, it has been said a thousand times, "Idle time is the devil's workshop."

Prayer

Place a fire in me, dear God, to work with passion for You. Let me use my time to Your honor and glory and convict me when I waste my time in idleness. Give me the wisdom to know the difference between slothfulness and relaxation and to act accordingly.

STAY IN THE RACE, CASE

"For some are already turned aside after Satan." 1 Timothy 5:15

Paul is addressing the care of widows in 1 Timothy 5. In verses 13-14, he is encouraging the younger widows to remain faithful to their commitment to Christ. He even went a step further and encouraged them to marry, have children and glorify God in the home. Sadly, some of them had cast off their faith and were now following Satan. The devil lured these young widows away from righteous lives into ungodly relationships. Simply put, they had dropped out of the Christian race.

Paul said in 1 Corinthians 15:57, *"But thanks be to God, which giveth us the victory through our Lord Jesus Christ."* Here we see that Christ has already run the race. Therefore, we don't have to win the race, all we have to do is stay in the race. Let me offer the following advice from Hebrews 12:1-2 for staying in the race. *First,* run by laying "aside every weight, and the sin…" The word "weight" refers to encumbrances such as ungodly associations, worldliness, bad habits, and the like. The "sin" spoken of here is not one sin in particular but whatever stops us from serving and living for the Lord. These things must be laid aside. *Second*, run the race "with patience." The word "patience" means "to abide beneath a heavy load." When trials and temptations are placed upon our backs, we should find our strength in the Lord and continue to stand beneath their weight. *Third*, run the race "looking unto Jesus the author and finisher of our faith." This means to look at Him in the Word of God and follow the example He set forth. Doing these things will keep us from following the devil and help us stay in the race, Case.

You cannot make progress in the Christian race if you are sitting on the sidelines.

Prayer

Dear Heavenly Father, please guide my feet and help me to run this race. Whenever I feel discouraged, give me the strength to endure in the race.

DON'T GET CAUGHT IN THE SNARE, BLAIR

"And that they may recover themselves out of the snare of the devil, who are taken captive by him at his will."
2 Timothy 2:26

Paul is admonishing believers who are walking in the truth to lovingly minister to those who fell prey to false teachers. He describes the victims of these false teachers as being in "the snare of the devil" and "taken captive by him at his will." The word "snare" comes from the Greek term *pagdios* and it means "that which fastens." In Paul's day, it was also the word used for a mousetrap.

In Proverbs 7 we read about a young man who had been seduced by a harlot and was caught in a trap. The end result of his dilemma was that he was like "*a fool [being led] to the correction of the stocks; Till a dart strike through his liver; as a bird hasteth to the snare, and knoweth not that it is for his life*" (Prov. 7:22-23). This young man found himself in the grasp of a trap with no ability to get free. The phrase "the correction of the stocks" was used for a criminal whose hands and feet were bound with chains or wood. The NIV substitutes the picture of a bound criminal with a "deer stepping into a noose." But what is even more frightening, in either case, the victim was trapped—waiting to take an arrow through the liver. He is also compared to a bird caught in a snare waiting to die. Woefully, this young man serves as an example of one who is in the snare of the devil.

In order to avoid falling into the devil's trap, there are three things we can learn from this young man's example in Proverbs 7. He descended into the wrong places (8-9), dealt with the wrong people (10-12), and desired the wrong pleasures (13-20). By learning from his example, you will not get caught in the snare, Blair.

Show me where you hang out, who you hang out with, and what pleasures you desire, and I will show you your end.

Prayer

Dear God, let me walk so close to You that I can spot the devil's traps way before I get close to them.

KEEP A TIGHT LIP, KIPP

"And the tongue is a fire, a world of iniquity: so is the tongue among our members, that it defileth the whole body, and seeth on fire the course of nature; and it is set on fire of hell." James 3:6

In James 3:1-12, the writers gives us an eloquent discourse on the power and destructive nature of the tongue. Physically speaking, the tongue is the movable muscle located in the bottom part of the mouth. It is covered with saliva and contains the taste buds. The tongue is also an essential aid in the pronunciation of words. Spiritually speaking, the tongue refers to the words that come out of a person's mouth. James said the tongue "is set on fire of hell." The word "hell" is the Greek word *Gehenna* and it was used to refer to a garbage dump outside the city of Jerusalem in Jesus' day. It was a place where a continual fire burned with rubbish and the bodies of dead animals and people. The reference to the tongue being set on fire of hell indicates it is a mighty tool of mass destruction in the hand of the devil. In this passage, James talks about the power of the tongue (3-6), the perversion of the tongue (7-8), and the produce of the tongue (9-12).

In order to overcome the destructive power of the tongue, I have developed the 5 D's for taming the tongue. *Dedicate* your tongue to the Lord (Rom. 12:1). *Devote* time daily in the Word to cleanse your tongue (Ps. 119:9). *Deny* the use of your tongue for sinful purposes (Rom. 6:12-13). *Develop* relationships with trusted friends who will be able to tell you when you offend with your tongue (Prov. 27:6). *Devaluate* your pride and accept the observations of others (Prov. 17:10). If you follow these 5 D's, they will help you keep a tight lip, Kipp.

"Ever wonder why God gave us two ears and one mouth, put our tongue behind a cage in water and put it no less than 6 inches from the brain?"
Author Unknown

Prayer

Set a guard, O Lord, over my mouth; keep watch over the door of my lips (Ps. 141:3). Keep my tongue from evil, and my lips from speaking guile (Ps. 34:13). Deliver my soul, O Lord, from lying lips, and from a deceitful tongue (Ps. 120:2). Because your lovingkindness is better than life, my lips shall praise thee (Ps. 63:3). My lips shall greatly rejoice when I sing unto thee (Ps. 71:23). Let the words of my mouth and the meditation of my heart, be acceptable in thy sight, O Lord, my strength, and my redeemer (Ps. 19:14).

SQUASH DISCORD, FORD

"But if ye have bitter envying and strife in your hearts, glory not, and lie not against the truth. This wisdom descendeth not from above, but is earthly, sensual, devilish. For where envying and strife is, there is confusion and every evil work."
James 3:14-16

James indicates that some people have strife in their hearts. The word "strife" comes from the Greek word *erithiah* and means "selfish ambition" but can also mean "faction, contention or divisions." Strife in the latter sense can be caused when a particular action triggers bitter feelings to arise between individuals or groups in the Body of Christ. The result is a separation where parties are at odds with one another. James draws our attention to the origin of this strife—it is "devilish." Satan sends out demons to do his evil work of causing division among the saints.

Sadly, strife can be devastating to relationships in the church. The Bible takes contention between God's people very seriously. Notice the following admonitions and warnings. *"Now I beseech you, brethren, mark them which* cause *divisions and offences contrary to the doctrine which ye have learned; and avoid them"* (Rom. 16:17). *"Now I beseech you, brethren, by the name of our Lord Jesus Christ, that ye all speak the same thing, and that there be no divisions among you; but that ye be perfectly joined together in the same mind and in the same judgment"* 1 Cor. 1:10). *"For ye are yet carnal: for whereas there is among you envying, and strife, and divisions, are ye not carnal, and walk as men?"* (1 Cor. 3:3). *"For first of all, when ye come together in the church, I hear that there be divisions among you; and I partly believe it. What shall I say to you? shall I praise you in this? I praise you not"* (1 Cor. 11:18, 22).

Believers should do their best to deal with conflict in a godly manner. We must understand when controversy is dealt with in unhealthy ways, we give Satan the upper hand. Some unhealthy ways to deal with conflict are—using threatening language, profanity, physical assaults, gossip, backbiting, or neglecting the issue. When the Word of God is followed, conflict can be worked out to His honor and glory. So squash discord, Ford.

"The Lord hates the one who sows discord among the brethren" (Prov. 6:19). Don't get on the Lord's hate list.

Prayer

Dear Jehovah Shalom, please use me to be an instrument of peace and not strife. Let me start by examining my heart for any bitterness and then become a peacemaker in Your Kingdom.

SUBMIT TO GOD, ROD

"Submit yourselves therefore to God. Resist the devil, and he will flee from you." James 4:7

James says to submit to God. The word submit comes from the Greek word *hupotasso* and is a military term meaning "to rank under." When believers take their rightful position under the authority of God [*their spiritual military officer*], they are naturally defended from the devil. To be submitted to God means to live according to the principles and precepts found in His Word.

There are speed limits in our country that drivers must obey. Some drivers believe they are above the law and go over the speed limit. At this point they are breaking the law and when caught breaking the law, they must suffer the consequences. The consequences can be a fine, points added to their insurance and in some cases incarceration. Likewise, when believers live above the laws of God, they will face certain consequences and they open themselves to Satan's influence. This is why it is important to submit to God, Rod.

A life that is submitted to God is a natural repellant to the devil.

Prayer

Dear God Almighty, give me the strength and the wisdom to live a life that is yielded and submitted to You.

THE DEVIL YOU MUST OPPOSE, ROSE

"Submit yourselves therefore to God. Resist the devil, and he will flee from you." James 4:7

After directing believers to submit themselves to God, James instructs them to resist the devil and he will flee from them. The word "resist" is the Greek term *anthisetmi*, which means "to stand against." The devil is on the attack and the believer must stand his ground. In Ephesians 6:13-17, God gives His children a suit of armor to stand against the devil.

The way to stand against the devil is to oppose a lie with the truth, oppose sin with righteousness, oppose turmoil with peace, oppose doubt with faith, oppose ignorance with knowledge, and oppose darkness with light.

When believers resist the devil, James says "he will flee from you." When Jesus resisted the devil in the wilderness, the Bible says, *"Then the devil leaveth him"* (Matt. 4:11). The word "leaveth" indicates that the devil left him alone on that occasion. Likewise, the devil will flee from believers when they resist him, but be assured that he will come back again. This is why the devil you must oppose, Rose, and it must be a continual practice.

The victory over the devil has already been won, we just have to stand until the battle is done.

Prayer

Dear Lord, I thank you for the victory over the devil, please give me the strength to stand against him.

DON'T LET YOUR PATIENCE WEAR THIN, KIN

"Behold, we count them happy which endure. Ye have heard of the patience of Job, and have seen the end of the Lord; that the Lord is very pitiful, and of tender mercy." James 5:11

Writing to encourage his readers to persevere in the midst of trials, James uses the ancient character Job as an example. We read back in the Book of Job, chapters one and two, that God granted the devil access to Job's life and he took his family, possessions and ultimately his health. In spite of this satanic affliction of great loss in his life, Job endured through his situation and God rewarded him in the end (Job 42:12). Job longed for God to appear, in order to have a hearing before Him (Job 23:3-5). Even though God did not show up right away, Job overcame the devil's attack with patient endurance.

In the New Testament there are two Greek terms for the word patience. The first is *makrothumia*, a compound word that comes from *makro*=long and *thumos*= temper. It carries the meaning of having a long temper or not getting heated quickly. The other term is another compound word—*hupomeno, hupo*=under, *meno*= to abide, which means "to abide underneath the load." This is the word used in James 5:11. When Job lost his possessions, family and health, he was still able to patiently endure through his losses because he had "patience" *hypomene* "the ability to abide underneath the load."

The best antidote for impatience is to have a plan to deal with it. One thing we can do is to know ourselves. We should be aware of the things that cause us to become impatient. Once those things are identified, we should follow the advice of the Apostle Paul who says we should put on a heart of patience (Col. 3:12). To put on a heart of patience means to know the things that cause impatience and implement strategies for overcoming them. Someone has said when we fail to plan, we plan to fail. If we don't have a plan to successfully deal with our impatience, it will defeat us every time. But if we do, our patience will not wear thin, Kin.

I had a church member who used to say, "Some people are like a newly-built hospital with empty beds—they need patients (patience)."

Prayer

Dear Heavenly Father, I must confess there are times in my life when I have been impatient. Please forgive me for being impatient and let me have the patience of Job. Let me be prepared for trying times by strengthening me with longsuffering.

BE ALERT, BURT

"Be sober, be vigilant; because your adversary the devil, as a roaring lion, walketh about, seeking whom he may devour." 1 Peter 5:8

The devil is seeking to devour the believer, which is why we are told to be sober and vigilant. The word "sober" carries with it the idea of having a clear and alert mind, while vigilant has to do with not being drowsy. In the case of the first word, it is linked with not altering your mind with any substance like alcohol or drugs, while the second word is related to getting enough sleep so that you are not dozing off. To have an inebriated or drowsy mind is to be open game for an attack by the devil.

There is a great danger on the American highways today and that is sleep impaired drivers. Those suffering from a deprivation of sleep are the cause of many road fatalities. The reason is they are not alert to signs and lights informing them to yield, stop, merge, or slow down. Because of their drowsiness, they drift over the white lines into the next lane or they cross over mediums into traffic coming from the other direction.

When believers are not sober or vigilant, they miss God's warning lights and drift into the path of the roaring lion, Satan. They are not aware they are wandering into the devil's lane or running into oncoming temptations. The believer must be alert, Burt, by staying sober, vigilant and having a discerning spirit that recognizes when the devourer is on the attack.

Animals not paying attention are easy prey for the lion.

Prayer

Lord, give me a keen ear to hear the roaring of the lion.

WATCH OUT FOR THE LION, BRIAN

"Be sober, be vigilant; because your adversary the devil, as a roaring lion, walketh about, seeking whom he may devour." 1 Peter 5:8

Peter compares the devil to a roaring lion seeking to devour its prey. This is a fitting analogy of Satan because he is trying to devour the people of God. This means he is trying to destroy their lives by getting them to fall into sin, obliterating their testimonies, or discouraging their hearts. Sad to say, this lion has many victims both within the pages of the Bible and outside of it. He devours individuals, relationships, families, churches, businesses and neighbors of every race, tribe and tongue.

It is important to recognize this devouring lion so that one does not end up in his jaws. God's people must realize what they have to lose when consumed by the devil. It might be a good idea right now for you to reflect upon how it would feel to be devoured by Satan. How would it feel to have to tell a spouse you love that you have been unfaithful? How would it feel to be caught by your employer viewing pornography?

How would it feel to be arrested for a crime with television cameras rolling in your face? How would it feel to be caught in a lie by someone you highly respect? In order to avoid feeling like this, you have to watch out for the lion, Brian.

Don't be like an animal caught in a trap, waiting to be devoured by the enemy.

Prayer

Dear Heavenly Father, help me to avoid snares set up by the enemy to consume my life, my testimony and my well-being!

PUT ON YOUR NIKE, MIKIE

"I write unto you, fathers, because ye have known him that is from the beginning. I write unto you, young men, because ye have overcome the wicked one. I write unto you, little children, because ye have known the Father. I have written unto you, fathers, because ye have known him that is from the beginning. I have written unto you, young men, because ye are strong, and the word of God abideth in you, and ye have overcome the wicked one." 1 John 2:13-14

Twice in these two verses the Apostle John said to his readers, "Ye have overcome the wicked one" (13-14). The word "overcome" derives from the Greek work *nikao*; this is where we get our English word NIKE, which is an athletic line of sportswear. The word *nikao* means to be victorious. The persons spoken of in these verses have the power to overcome the evil one, who is the devil.

I often hear Christians say, "I am trying to get the victory." My response to that is there is bad news and good news. The bad news is no matter how hard you try, you cannot get the victory. The good news is Jesus Christ has already won the victory, *"But thanks be to God, which giveth us the victory through our Lord Jesus Christ"* (1 Cor. 15:57). As believers, we don't have to try to win the victory, all we have to do is walk in it. There is no legitimate reason for a child of God to labor under ongoing discouragement and defeat inflicted by the devil. When Satan buffets us, we may have to get alone with God in our prayer closet. But when we emerge out of the secret place, it should be with renewed zeal and vigor to walk in victory. This is why you should put on your Nike, Mikie.

God does not call us to win the race, He calls us to stay in the race.

Prayer

Thank You for the victory, Lord! Always help me to remember that I am an overcomer through Jesus Christ.

PURPOSE TO SIN LESS, JESS

"He that committeth sin is of the devil;
for the devil sinneth from the beginning."
1 John 3:8

As children of God, believers are called to live righteous lives. One day we will come face to face with Jesus and we will be like Him in sinless perfection. This should be great motivation for us to cleanse ourselves from sin. The difference between a child of God and a child of the devil is the child of God should purpose to live a righteous life. When a believer lives a life of sin, he is acting more like a child of the devil who was a sinner from the very beginning.

On the day when we stand before Jesus, "we shall be like him; for we shall see him as he is" (1 John 3:2). The transformation of being like Jesus on the day we see Him will be great for some and minor for others. It will be a great renovation for those who did not live a life dedicated to righteousness; and minor for those who pursued holiness. In order to live a life that transforms us more and more into the image of Jesus, you have to purpose to sin less, Jess.

On the day when you see Jesus, will your transformation be a light touch-up or an extreme makeover?

Prayer

Lord, give me wisdom and strength to walk in Your ways, and help me to sin less each and every day.

OVERCOME HATE, NATE

"Not as Cain, who was of that wicked one, and slew his brother. And wherefore slew he him? Because his own works were evil, and his brother's righteous."
1 John 3:12

Cain killed his brother Abel because he was influenced by the wicked one, the devil. A few verses later John says, "Whosoever hateth his brother is a murderer" (15). From the previous information we can arrive at three conclusions: Cain hated his brother, he was a murderer, and he was influenced by the devil. Jesus leads us to believe that anger and hatred are at the center of killing another person (Matt. 5:21-22). Hatred is straight from the pit of hell. Anyone whose heart is filled with hate is definitely influenced by Satan.

There are many Christians who feel they have the right to hate other people because they were wounded deeply by them. This is a wrong attitude and it gives the devil a place to enter in and do his destructive work. Hate is a word that should not be mentioned in the believer's vocabulary unless it is hatred for evil deeds. Whether he is saved, unsaved or even if that person has committed a dastardly offense against all of humanity, a child of God should not hate another person. God's message to His people is love—love your spouse (Eph. 5:25), love your friends (John 15:12-17), and love your enemies (Matt. 5:44). As believers we must be on the lookout for any root of hatred springing up in our hearts. At the first sign of hatred in our hearts, we must come to the Lord and ask Him to help us deal with it. In doing so, you can overcome hate, Nate.

Martin Luther King, Jr. said, "Let no man pull you so low as to hate him."

Prayer

Lord, help me to understand that my sins sent Your Son, whom You loved with Your whole heart, to die on the cross. Yet in spite of this, You have loved and forgiven me. Help me not to hold hatred in my heart for anyone.

NO NEED TO FEAR,
MY DEAR

*"Ye are of God, little children, and have
overcome them: because greater is he that
is in you, than he that is in the world."*
1 John 4:4

In 1 John 4, the apostle is warning his
readers about false teachers who had the spirit
of the antichrist. John assures believers that they
have overcome them because they are of God.
The literally Greek reading of "Ye are of God"
is "You are out of God." This means they were
positionally in God, and God was in them
through the indwelling of the Holy Spirit.
Because of this, they had no need to fear for they
were more than conquerors through Jesus Christ
and able to overcome the spirit of antichrist.
Then John concludes, "Greater is He who is in
you [God], than he who is in the world [Satan]."

Whatever the circumstances, the child of
God has no reason to fear. Someone has said that
F-E-A-R is False Evidence Appearing Real. I
would like to offer the following principles
for overcoming fear. First, keep yourself in the
presence of the Lord (Ps. 91:1-7), His presence
drives fear away. Second, meditate on the fact that

the Lord is on your side and you have nothing to fear (Ps. 27:1). Third, take advantage of the resources God has given you to combat fear— supernatural power, the assurance of God's loving presence and the ability to discipline yourself to overcome fear (2 Tim. 1:7). Fourth, face your fear with authority (Ps. 23:4). Take practical steps to overcome your fear by asking yourself the following questions: What is the cause of my fear? What is the worst thing my fear can do to me? What is my fear keeping me from doing? What are the benefits of me overcoming my fear? What is the first little thing I can do to face my fear? If you follow these principles, there is no need to fear, my dear.

"The only thing we have to fear is fear itself."
Franklin D. Roosevelt

Prayer

Heavenly Father, I thank You that Christ's resurrection out of the grave not only provides victory over death but it also includes victory over fear. Lord, please help me deal with my fear. Help me to identify the thing that causes my fear to be aroused and how it is affecting my life. Father, give me the strength and the knowledge to follow the principles for overcoming fear.

LET THE LORD REBUKE, LUKE

"Yet Michael the archangel, when contending with the devil he disputed about the body of Moses, durst not bring against him a railing accusation, but said, The Lord rebuke thee." Jude 9

In the Book of Deuteronomy, we read when Moses died that he was buried in the land of Moab and *"no man knoweth of his sepulcher unto this day"* (Deut. 34:5-6). According to a Jewish tradition, there was an argument between Michael the Archangel and the devil about the remains of Moses. As powerful as Michael is, he did not dispute with the devil over Moses' body but said, "The Lord rebuke thee."

As believers, we have not been called to engage the devil personally. We are told to resist him, flee from him, and stand against him. We should not go out looking to pick a fight with the devil; but if we find ourselves in a confrontation with him, we should submit ourselves to God and resist him. Believers have no ability to fight against the devil or demons in their own strength. But we have all the power we need when we stand behind the Lord, so let Him do the rebuke, Luke.

Don't get into an argument with the devil on your own; you will lose because he is a great debater.

Prayer

Father, the devil would love nothing more than for me to engage him in a personal debate. Please give me the wisdom to realize that one word from You will take him down.

WATCH OUT FOR
SATAN'S THRONE,
STONE

"I know thy works, and where thou dwellest, even where Satan's seat is."
Revelation 2:13

Christ, in writing to the church of Pergamum, told them He was aware of the fact the church was located in a city that was the center of Satan's seat. The word seat comes from the Greek term thronos, which means throne. This informs us that the city was a place of Satan's throne or where he ruled. Several theories have been offered as to the identification of Satan's throne, but the key understanding to glean from this phrase is that it was a place dominated by evil.

As people of God, we must realize there are certain places we must avoid because they are purely evil. For the believer, Satan's throne can be a movie theatre playing an ungodly movie, a music concert where the band uses profanity and derogatory remarks about females, a bar with male or female strippers, or any event or place that provides an environment for people to get sloppy drunk. Paul wrote in 1 Corinthians

15:33, "*Do not be so deceived and misled! Evil companionships (communion, associations) corrupt and deprave good manners and morals and character*" (AMP). This is why it is important to watch out for Satan's throne, Stone.

Someone has said, devil without the d is evil.

Prayer

Dear Most Gracious Lord, I repeat the words of Jesus in this prayer, "Lead me not into temptation but deliver me from evil."

BE CAUTIOUS OF THE REPROACH, COACH

"And I heard a loud voice saying in heaven, Now is come salvation, and strength, and the kingdom of our God, and the power of his Christ: for the accuser of our brethren is cast down, which accused them before our God day and night." Revelation 12:10

The devil stands against all that God represents. If he could, he would love to take God down or at least bring an accusation against Him. Since God is a perfect and holy being, this will never happen so the devil goes for the next best thing—the believer. Whenever he can cause a believer to stumble, he runs to the Lord and whoever else to make it known that one of God's people has fallen into sin. This is why he is called "the accuser of our brethren." Sad to say, every day there are pastors, leaders and members in the Body of Christ who are falling prey to Satan's tactics.

As we peruse the pages of the Bible, we see many of God's choice servants who the devil had the opportunity to bring accusations against.

Adam ate the forbidden fruit, Moses struck the rock instead of speaking to it, Abraham lied about Sarah being his wife, Samson was seduced by Delilah, David committed adultery with Bathsheba, Peter denied Christ, and the list goes on. Let me offer the following advice to avoid being a victim of Satan's accusations. First, live a life of moral integrity; be holy in public and in private. Second, go to the source of any misinformation that may be circulating about you. The devil not only loves to run with true accusations, but sometimes he runs faster with false allegations. Third, come before the Lord daily and lay your life out before Him. In doing this, He will keep you sensitive to anything in your life that might bring reproach, Coach.

The mud of accusations cannot stick on the walls of your life if you keep your temple clean.

Prayer

Search me, oh God, and know my heart: try me and know my thoughts: And see if there be any wicked way in me, and lead me in the way everlasting.

DON'T ACCEPT THE GUILT, WILT

"And I heard a loud voice saying in heaven, Now is come salvation, and strength, and the kingdom of our God, and the power of his Christ: for the accuser of our brethren is cast down, which accused them before our God day and night." Revelation 12:10

In this verse Satan is identified as "the accuser of our brethren." This is right in line with his name, Satan, which means "adversary or accuser." We read in Ephesians 6:11 that he has many tricks and one of his tricks is to get God's people to accuse themselves. The end result of this is a tool used by him called guilt. This is where he keeps his victim in bondage to feelings of condemnation and hopelessness. The causes of guilt can be: failure to do something one was supposed to do, failure to meet certain expectations (set by family, employer, church, etc.), committing a moral failure, committing a sin which one feels cannot be forgiven, and accepting responsibility for something bad that happened which was beyond one's control. Even though these might have occurred, let me offer four steps for breaking this satanic stronghold. First, identify the cause of your guilt (Ps. 51:3). Second, confess (if necessary) and accept God's forgiveness (1 John. 1:9). Third, forgive yourself (if necessary) and realize you are accepted by God (Eph. 1:6). Fourth, if you are having a problem overcoming guilt, seek help from an experienced believer or biblical counselor (Prov. 24:6). Practice using these four steps so that you don't accept the guilt, Wilt.

Guilt is from Satan and conviction is from the Holy Spirit. Ask the Lord to help you discern the difference.

Prayer

Dear God, help me to realize the reality of Romans 8:1 that there is no condemnation to them which are in Christ Jesus, and help me to walk in the deliverance from guilt rooted in a relationship with Christ.

OVERCOME WITH YOUR STORY, CORY

"And they overcame him [the dragon, that old serpent, called the Devil, and Satan] by the blood of the Lamb, and by the word of their testimony; and they loved not their lives unto the death."
Revelation 12:11

In this verse we see a group of victors who overcame Satan "by the word of their testimony." The testimony of these individuals is that they were committed to Christ. In the midst of persecution by Satan, they did not waver but remained faithful to their testimony. In Revelation 6:9, we read about some martyred saints who held on to their commitment to Christ even to the point of death.

As followers of Jesus Christ, we have a story, which is the testimony of our commitment to Him. The devil will try to shake our commitment to Christ. Throughout the Scriptures, we see God's people being tested in the area of their commitment. Joseph was tested by Potiphar's wife (Gen. 39:7-12), the three Hebrew boys were thrown into the fiery furnace (Dan. 3:1-30),

Daniel was placed into the den of lions (Dan. 6:1-28), Paul and Silas were beaten and placed into prison (Acts 16:22-31), and the saints, beheaded during the Tribulation (Rev. 20:4). Let's look at what they did to hold on to their commitment—they fled from evil, they refused to worship other gods, they maintained their dedication to God's Word and prayer, they refused to keep silent about their devotion to Christ, they sang praises in the midst of persecution, and they remained faithful to their God. The next time Satan tries to shake your commitment to Christ, overcome him with your story, Corey.

The devil is a thief; don't let him steal your testimony.

Prayer

Father, when I am attacked and persecuted from every direction, give me strength to hold fast to my testimony.

IT IS NOT ABOUT SELF, ELF

*"And they overcame him by the blood
of the Lamb, and by the word of their
testimony; and they loved not their lives
unto the death."* Revelation 12:11

Just prior to this verse, we read about
Satan being ousted from Heaven. In verse 12
John writes, "Woe to the inhabiters of the earth
and of the sea! For the devil is come down unto
you, having great wrath, because he knoweth that
he hath but a short time." The devil is furious
because he has been banished from Heaven and
in his rage, he is trying to take down as many
people as he can. But there was a group of
believers that overcame him. Notice how they
did it, "by the blood of the Lamb, and by the
word of their testimony; and they loved not their
lives unto the death." In the triplet of overcoming
principles found in verse 11, we want to focus
specifically on the last one, "they loved not their
lives unto the death." When Satan persecuted
these individuals, he thought that he defeated
them. However, they overcame him, even though
some of them died, because they loved not their
life even to the point of death. This ultimate act

of dying to self enabled them to overcome Satan.

Most Christians in the world may not have to face persecution like these saints did, so we might ask the question, "What does dying to 'self' look like to them?" I found the following reading in my archives entitled "*Dying to Self.*" I am not sure of its origin.

When you are forgotten, neglected, or purposely set at naught, and don't sting and hurt with the insult of over sight, but your heart is happy, THAT IS DYING TO SELF.

When your good is evil spoken of, when your wishes are crossed, your advice disregarded, your opinions ridiculed, and you refuse to let anger rise in your heart, or even defend yourself, but take it all in patient, loving silence, THAT IS DYING TO SELF.

When you can receive correction and reproof from one of less stature than yourself and can humbly submit inwardly as well as outwardly, find no rebellion or resentment rising within your heart, THAT IS DYING TO SELF.

So you see to overcome Satan, it is not about self, Elf. What does dying to "self" mean to you?

Prayer

Lord, give me the wisdom and knowledge to overcome self for in doing so I am also overcoming Satan.

LET YOUR AROMA ALWAYS SMELL SWEET, PETE

"And unto the angel of the church in Smyrna write; These things saith the first and the last, which was dead, and is alive; I know thy works, and tribulation, and poverty, (but thou art rich) and I know the blasphemy of them which say they are Jews, and are not, but are the synagogue of Satan. Fear none of those things which thou shalt suffer: behold, the devil shall cast some of you into prison, that ye may be tried; and ye shall have tribulation ten days: be thou faithful unto death, and I will give thee a crown of life. He that hath an ear, let him hear what the Spirit saith unto the churches; He that overcometh shall not be hurt of the second death." Revelation 2:8-10

In these verses we read about a church that suffered intense persecution at the hand of Satan. He may have used people as his instruments of persecution, but he was the director of it. The church at the brunt of this persecution was the Church in Smyrna. The name Smyrna means "myrrh", this was a plant that emitted a sweet fragrance (Ps. 45:8; Prov. 7:17; Song of Sol 3:6). I preached a sermon from this passage titled Crushed Flowers Give off a Sweet Aroma. It was centered on the idea that when this church was crushed by Satan, with the torment of being cast into prison, they should reflect the character of their name and give off a sweet aroma. Likewise, when believers find themselves in the crucible of persecution they should emit the fragrance of Christ. Below I have listed some ways for God's people to deal with persecution:

When you are pounded by the hammer
of criticism—emit a sweet aroma and
don't criticize back.

When you are squashed under the foot of
mistreatment—emit a sweet aroma and forgive.

When you are squeezed in the press,
being hurt—emit a sweet aroma and
go to the offender.

When you are mashed under the anvil of
false accusation—emit a sweet aroma and
keep loving your accusers.

When you are pressed in the vat of

condemnation—emit a sweet aroma and maintain your testimony.

By doing these things, you can let your aroma always smell sweet, Pete.

I heard someone say, "The teapot sings its best when it is up to neck in hot water and the rubber band is most effective when it is stretched to its limits."

Prayer

Dear God of All Comfort. Thank You for being with me during my times of crushing! Help me stay strong and throughout the process of me being crushed, allow me to emit the fragrance of Christ!

TRIUMPH OVER THE SYNAGOGUE OF SATAN, PEYTON

"I know thy works, and tribulation, and poverty, (but thou are rich) and I know the blasphemy of them which say they are Jews, and are not, but are the synagogue of Satan." Revelation 2:9

Christ is writing to the church in Smyrna, one of the seven churches in Asia Minor listed in Revelation chapters two and three. The verse above causes concern because it talks about a group of blasphemers who were of the synagogue of Satan. But what is even more troubling are the words found in verse 10, "behold, the devil shall cast some of you into prison, that ye may be tried; and ye shall have tribulation ten days..." The devil is described as bringing great persecution and suffering upon some of the saints in this church. However, despite this Satanic oppression Jesus encouraged them with the following words, "be faithful unto death, and I will give thee a crown of life" (10). In this verse, Christ is calling for faithfulness from the saints.

The word faithful comes from the Greek word pistos and it means "trustworthy, steadfast, loyal or consistent." The meaning which seems to be the best fit for the context of this passage is loyal. The story is told of a Christian cemetery with an unusual statue in it. This statue is not of an angel, saint, man or woman. It is the statue of a dog. Many people wonder how the statue got there. It is said, that a man passed away and during the motorcade to the cemetery, his dog dutifully followed the procession. After the graveyard workers buried the man the dog diligently stood by the owner' grave until he died. As a result of the dog's devotion to his master, a statue was erected in honor of his loyalty. This dog serves as a good example to believers, he was loyal to his dead master. Christians, however, are called to show their allegiance to a living Master.

Loyalty to Christ involves two key things: an unselfish allegiance to Him (Mk. 8:34) and a commitment to proclaim and live out the Gospel (Mk. 8:35; Rom. 1:16) in the face of persecution. As we move into the future, attacks against the Word of God and the Christ faith will increase intensely. This is why it is important to remember—loyalty to Christ triumphs over the synagogue of Satan, Peyton.

Loyalty to Christ is not tested in times of calm and coziness, but in times of adversity and antagonism.

Prayer

Dear God Almighty, I thank You for Your loyalty to me. The Bible presents You as a loving God who is loyal to us through the most adverse conditions. I pray that You give me the wisdom, awareness and conviction to be loyal to You when I am persecuted for Your sake.

STAND ON THE WORD, BYRD

"But he answered and said, It is written, Man shall not live by bread alone, but by every word that proceedeth out of the mouth of God."
Matthew 4:4

In the Greek language there are two words used for the English term "word." One is the word logos and it refers to the entire revealed Word of God. The other word is rhema and it refers to a specific word activated in the heart of a believer by the Holy Spirit.

When Jesus was tempted by Satan in the wilderness, He responded to the first temptation with the words, "It is written, Man shall not live by bread alone, but by every word rhema that proceedeth out of the mouth of God" (Matt. 4:4). Like Jesus, the believer should learn how to fight the devil with the rhema of God. Here's how to stand on the Word Byrd:

When the devil hits you with poverty,
hit him with Psalm 37:25:
*"I have been young, and now am old;
yet have I not seen the righteous forsaken,
nor his seed begging bread."*

When the devil hits you with discouragement,
hit him with Psalm 42:5:
*"Why art thou cast down, O my soul? and why
art thou disquieted in me? hope thou in God:
for I shall yet praise him for the help of his
countenance."*

When the devil hits you with evil thoughts,
hit him with Philippians: 4:8:
*"Finally, brethren, whatsoever things are true,
whatsoever things are honest, whatsoever things
are just, whatsoever things are pure, whatsoever
things are lovely, whatsoever things are of good
report; if there be any virtue, and if there be any
praise, think on these things."*

When the devil hits you with anger,
hit him with Ephesians 4:26:
*"Be ye angry, and sin not: let not the sun go
down upon your wrath:"*

When the devil hits you with taking revenge,
hit him with Romans 12:19:
*"Dearly beloved, avenge not yourselves, but
rather give place unto wrath: for it is written,
Vengeance is mine; I will repay, saith the Lord."*

When the devil hits you with a desire to gossip,
hit him with Psalm 141:3:

"Set a watch, O LORD, before my mouth; keep the door of my lips."

When the devil hits you with fear,
hit him with Psalm 27:1:
"The LORD is my light and my salvation; whom shall I fear? the LORD is the strength of my life; of whom shall I be afraid?"

When the devil hits you with loneliness,
hit him with Proverbs 18:24:
"A man that hath friends must shew himself friendly: and there is a friend that sticketh closer than a brother."

When the devil hits you with temptation,
hit him with 1 Corinthians 10:13:
"There hath no temptation taken you but such as is common to man: but God is faithful, who will not suffer you to be tempted above that ye are able; but will with the temptation also make a way to escape, that ye may be able to bear it."

When the devil hits you with illness,
hit him with Psalm 34:1:
"I will bless the LORD at all times: his praise shall continually be in my mouth."

The Word of God does not become a rhema until it is activated in the heart.

Prayer

Dear Lord of Hosts, thank you for giving me Your rhemas to stand against Satan. Let me spend time meditating in Your Word in order to know what it says, so that I might be able to stand on it in the heat of the battle against the enemy.

UNDERSTAND THE MEANING OF HIS NAME, MAME

What's in a name? There are many designations for Satan in the Bible. These designations not only reflect his character but also his mode of operation. Listed below are some of his names and what they mean. The only other person who has more names than Satan is Jesus Christ.

Accuser of our brethren - Revelation 12:10
"One who points a finger at the righteous when they fall"

Angel of light - 2 Corinthians 11:14-15
"Deceptive ability to look beautiful and righteous"

Apollyon - Revelation 9:11
"The destroyer"

Beelzebub - Matthew 12:24
"Lord of the flies or prince of demons"

Belial - 2 Corinthians 6:15
"Vile, ruthless or worthless one"

141

Deceiver - Revelation 20:10
*"One who can trick others into
doing wickedness"*

Devil - Matthew 4:1; Revelation 12:9
"Slanderer"

Dragon - Revelation 12:7
"Ability to terrify"

Enemy - Matthew 13:39
*"The one who opposes all that is
righteous and godly"*

God of this world - 2 Corinthians 4:4
"Ruler of this present time"

Potentate of death - Hebrews 2:14
*"The one who inflicts physical, spiritual
and eternal death"*

Liar - John 8:44
"Author of all that is untrue"

Lucifer - Isaiah 14:12
"Morning star, shining or bright one"

Murderer - John 8:44
"One who is the author of physical death"

Old serpent - Revelation 20:2
"The one who deceived Eve"

Prince of the power of the air - Ephesians. 2:2
"Authority in the heavens"

Prince of this world - John 12:31
"His reign in the hearts of the unsaved"

Roaring lion - 1 Peter 5:8
"One who is able to devour"

Satan - Job 1:6; John. 13:27; Acts 5:3
"Adversary"

Tempter - 1 Thessalonians 3:5
*"The one who lures people from
the right way"*

Wicked one - Matthew 13:38
"The author of evil"

To resist the wiles of the devil, understand the meaning of his name, Mame.

SUBJECT INDEX

SCRIPTURE INDEX

CONTACT INFORMATION

Dr. William R. Glaze
Bethany Baptist Church
7745 Tioga Street
Pittsburgh, PA 15208
412.242.3255
pwrglaze@aol.com

OTHER WORKS BY DR. WILLIAM R. GLAZE

Laying a Firm Foundation for the Covenant of Marriage: Helping Engaged Couples Prepare for the Covenant of Marriage

Bible Prophecy: A Look into God's Plans for the Future

Rebuilding the Fences of Broken Relationships: A Study in the Book of Philemon

Discipleship for New Believers: Spiritual Food for Babes in Christ from the Land of Milk and Honey

Touched by the Breath of God: All Scripture is Given by Inspiration of God

153

Made in the USA
San Bernardino, CA
22 October 2016